I0441962

Army Equipment Program

in support of

President's Budget 2016

Foreword

Our Army remains the absolute foundation of the Joint Force, and our allies and partners not only look for us to lead, they expect us to lead. Today, our Total Army is significantly and simultaneously committed on six continents, in places such as South Korea, the Philippines, and Japan, in Turkey, Qatar, Jordan, and Kuwait, in Latvia, Estonia, Poland, Romania, and Lithuania, and in Central and South America. We are committed in Africa in Djibouti, Mali, Nigeria, and Guinea. We are recommitting advise and assist forces in Iraq to counter the Islamic State of Iraq and the Levant threat and the Army remains engaged in Afghanistan.

Yet even with the increasing velocity of instability around the world, the Army's modernization budget has been reduced every year since Fiscal Year (FY) 2011. This year's budget preserves options for the future by protecting science and technology, preserves Total Army near-term readiness through upgrades and procurement of existing programs and accepts risk in the mid-term by postponing new development.

Equipping the Army to deploy rapidly around the world provides our nation with unmatched capabilities to win, translating military objectives into enduring political outcomes. Equipment modernization provides combatant commanders with globally responsive Army formations capable of expeditionary maneuver that can rapidly transition into operations with campaign level endurance. After more than a decade of rapid equipping focused on adding protection, Army modernization efforts are restoring the appropriate balance of mobility, protection, and lethality to Army formations as required by their mission sets, in order to overmatch current and future threats.

Predictable and consistent funding is required to modernize on the current timeline, meet the evolving threat and fully execute Defense Strategic Guidance requirements. The cumulative cuts in modernization programs threaten to cede our current overmatch of potential adversaries while increasing future costs to regain or maintain parity if lost. If sequestration returns as scheduled in FY 2016, the tough choices and gains we've already made will be eroded and the Army will be at grave risk of fully executing the Defense Strategic Guidance requirements.

Raymond T. Odierno
General, United States Army

John M. McHugh
Secretary of the Army

Table of Contents

Foreword

TABLE OF FIGURES

Executive Summary

"I think both the President and the Secretary of Defense have made very clear that their main objective, which is ours as well, is to preserve this magnificent land force that's been built over the last 10 years, and ensure we remain in the future what we are today: the greatest land power the world's ever seen."[1]

The Army, as part of joint, interorganizational, and multinational teams, provides multiple options to the Nation's leadership, integrates multiple partners and operates across multiple domains to present adversaries with multiple dilemmas and achieve sustainable outcomes. The complexity of future armed conflict will require well equipped and modernized Total Army forces capable of conducting missions in the homeland or in foreign lands. Army mission sets require stable funding that ensure the ability of the Army to modernize the force with the best commercial and government developed technologies.

The Army's funding for equipment modernization enters a critical time frame. This year's budget represents Total Army equipment modernization during a period where the operational and fiscal environments are straining Army efforts to balance modernization to meet current demands while building the foundations of a force that can meet future challenges. Over the past several years the Army has absorbed significant reductions in Research, Development and Acquisition (RDA) accounts.

As the RDA accounts shrink, the Army will have to consider significant restructure of over 80 acquisition programs when Budget Control Act funding levels return in fiscal year 2016. The program restructures will include delaying new starts, reducing current system modernization upgrades and cancelling some programs. The reduction in RDA accounts is occurring at a time of increasing demand for Army Forces around the world due to regional instability, e.g., Ukraine, Syria, Iraq and North Korea and places our Soldiers at risk while increasing the potential for mission failure.

The Army is taking three steps to minimize the effect of reduced RDA funding on equipment modernization. First, the Army successfully protected our Science and Technology (S&T) funding at President's Budget (PB) 2015 levels. Protecting S&T helps maintain the Army's future overmatch capabilities in the mid to far term. Next, the Army is carefully reducing the number and pace of new systems in development to meet budget parameters while accepting the risk of reduced operational overmatch. Finally, we continue to develop and improve current equipment components, systems, and sub-systems to enhance capabilities albeit at a slower modernization rate.

---

[1] John M. McHugh, Secretary of the Army, Soldier's Magazine, June 2012.

The Army must also repair equipment returning from theaters to rebuild unit readiness. After our combat involvement in Afghanistan is complete, the Army will require supplemental funding for three years to reset equipment from the harsh demands of war. Any extensions of life for existing systems will increase Operations and Maintenance sustainment bills until modernization investments are renewed. The Army must also aggressively divest of equipment that is obsolete, not economically feasible to repair, non-standard or excess to need.

Helping guide the Army into the future is the new Force 2025 and Beyond plan that integrates and synchronizes Army adaptation, evolution, and innovation to develop the force within the realities of the fiscal and operational environments. Force 2025 and Beyond will identify and recommend opportunities to resource the highest operational value capabilities to fundamentally redirect and compress acquisition of key programs, similar to Army actions which produced the "Big Five"[2] in the late 1970's and 1980's. Among these capabilities is the need to provide the right balance of lethality, mobility and protection across each of the Brigade Combat Team formations to restore overmatch and avoid losing a differential advantage over adversaries. Initial insights indicate the need to develop requirements necessary to field a Mobile Protected Firepower vehicle, Ultra Light Combat Vehicle, Light Reconnaissance Vehicle and invest in S&T for the Future Fighting Vehicle and other key future programs.

The portfolio annexes to this document detail where we have applied our resources in FY 2016. Each portfolio has identified areas of risk created by reduced funding but has also addressed their ability to balance risk against funding, schedule, and capability to provide Soldiers and units with the most critical battlefield systems. We will prioritize our efforts to modernize the Network, with a goal of agile and expeditionary tactical command posts supported by robust home station architecture, to facilitate the decision-making of Soldiers with information and connectivity across all tactical echelons in support of the Joint Force and our multiple partners. Likewise, programming for ground vehicles such as the Army's critical Armored Multi-Purpose Vehicle (AMPV), Paladin Integrated Management (PIM) and Joint Light Tactical Vehicle (JLTV) are significant priorities. Similarly, Aviation reflects priorities for Apache, Black Hawk and Chinook helicopters as our most capable and survivable combat-proven aircraft. Additionally, we protect critical S&T investments as the seed corn for the future. However, achieving the Army's priority efforts will take more time due to the decline in resources for the RDA accounts. The Army will begin to recover the balance among modernization, readiness and manpower in FY 2020 as end strength stabilizes.

---

[2] Big Five is a popular reference to the Army's development of the Abrams main battle tank, the Bradley fighting vehicle, the Apache helicopter, the Patriot air defense system and the Black Hawk helicopter.

Linking Resource Decisions to Army Strategy

"Plans are worthless, but planning is everything."[3]

Overview:

The Army Equipment Program in support of the President's Budget 2016 (AEP PB 16) describes the Army RDA budget for key capability portfolio areas and the S&T portion of the Fiscal Year 2016 President's Budget request. The AEP PB 16 flows from the recent Army Equipment Modernization Strategy revision and the 2015 Army Equipment Program in support of the President's Budget 2015. This document delineates RDA investments into 11 capability portfolio areas, highlights the portfolio accomplishments over the last two years and provides intent for FY 2016 investments. The dollars and quantities in this document reflect President's Budget 2016.

Total Army equipment modernization enters a critical funding year. This year's budget represents Total Army equipment modernization during a period where the operational and fiscal environments are straining Army efforts to balance modernization to meet current demands while building the foundations of a force that can meet future challenges. Over the past several years the Army has absorbed significant reductions in RDA accounts increasing risk to Soldiers as the velocity of instability increases around the world. When Budget Control Act (BCA) of 2011 levels of funding return in FY 2016 the Army will be vulnerable to delay, restructure or termination of over 80 acquisition programs, particularly large ones.

Trends in threats, the operating environment, and technology highlight the enduring need for ready Army forces operating as part of joint, interorganizational, and multinational teams to prevent conflict, shape security environments, and win in a complex world. Enemies, adversaries, and individual threats make future armed conflict complex. The Army's competitive advantages in the land, air, maritime, space, and cyberspace domains are challenged by elusive and capable combatants. Advanced technologies will transfer readily to state and nonstate actors imposing costly capability gap solutions on the Total Army. The complexity of future armed conflict will require Army forces capable of conducting missions in the homeland or in foreign lands including defense support of civil authorities, international disaster relief and humanitarian assistance, security cooperation activities, crisis response, or large-scale operations to be well equipped and modernized. Army forces have long been essential to preventing conflict through the forward positioning or rotation of forces overseas.

---

[3] Dwight D. Eisenhower, Remarks at the National Defense Executive Reserve Conference, November 14, 1957

Regionally engaged Army forces are needed to build partner capability, assure allies, and deter adversaries. The Department of Defense (DoD) requires the Army, as part of the Joint Force, to deploy credible and reliable combined arms capabilities across the range of military operations. To prevent conflict, shape security environments and win wars in a complex world, Army forces will be essential for projecting national power through support for diplomatic, political, law enforcement, economic development, and other efforts.

The Force 2025 and Beyond effort integrates and synchronizes Total Army adaptation, evolution, and innovation over the near, mid, and far term to develop the force within the constraints of policy and the realities of the fiscal and operational environments. The Force 2025 plan nests within and informs The Army Plan and the Army Operating Concept Framework. While existing programs support emerging elements of Force 2025 and Beyond, the near-term efforts provide an opportunity to continue to learn through Force 2025 Maneuvers, analyze Warfighting Challenges for new or modified solutions, and implement improvements to Army Warfighting Functions.

Our equipment modernization approach is to focus on supporting our Soldiers and small unit formations, while maintaining the capacity to deter and defeat potential adversaries by identifying achievable requirements, applying best practices in acquisition and sustainment, seeking incremental improvements, and harnessing network enabled capabilities to solve near-term capability gaps; while investing in military-unique revolutionary and evolutionary technologies to solve future capability gaps. To achieve these ends for Soldiers and small unit formations, the Army must ensure combined arms formations possess the appropriate balance of lethality, mobility, and protection to accomplish the mission. The Army will emphasize long range planning to define future decision points that consider equipment age, degradation of overmatch abilities, technology advances, industrial base viability and closure of capability gaps in near (FY 2016), mid (FY 2017-2021) and far term (FY 2022-2031) timeframes aligning with the Five Year Development Plan (FYDP) and Extended Planning Period (EPP), while allowing for cost-informed decisions that balance force generation needs with the Total Force modernization posture.

The President's Budget 2016 represents the culmination of a significant and sustained collaborative effort by the Army to produce an efficient, balanced program that best serves the Nation's needs under severe fiscal constraints. Once again, the Army sized its force under funding levels for what it could afford, not what the Army believes our Nation needs to execute the Defense Strategy. The manpower program, readiness programs (training, installations, and sustainment), and capital investments program all experience near-term challenges while the Army reduces its military and civilian manpower. This Budget has required extremely difficult decisions and will require the support of Office of Secretary of Defense, Office of Management and Budget and Congress to remain viable. A return to BCA funding levels in FY 2016 will drive the Total Army to a 920K force that is unable to meet the Defense Strategy and will have severely degraded readiness levels beyond 2020. Despite the inherent difficulty in operating under this level of fiscal uncertainty, the Army will continue to seek innovative means of providing highly capable rotational land forces to combatant commanders. The force we have, while being too small, will be rotationally focused and surge ready.

Strategic Priorities for Ready and Modern Army

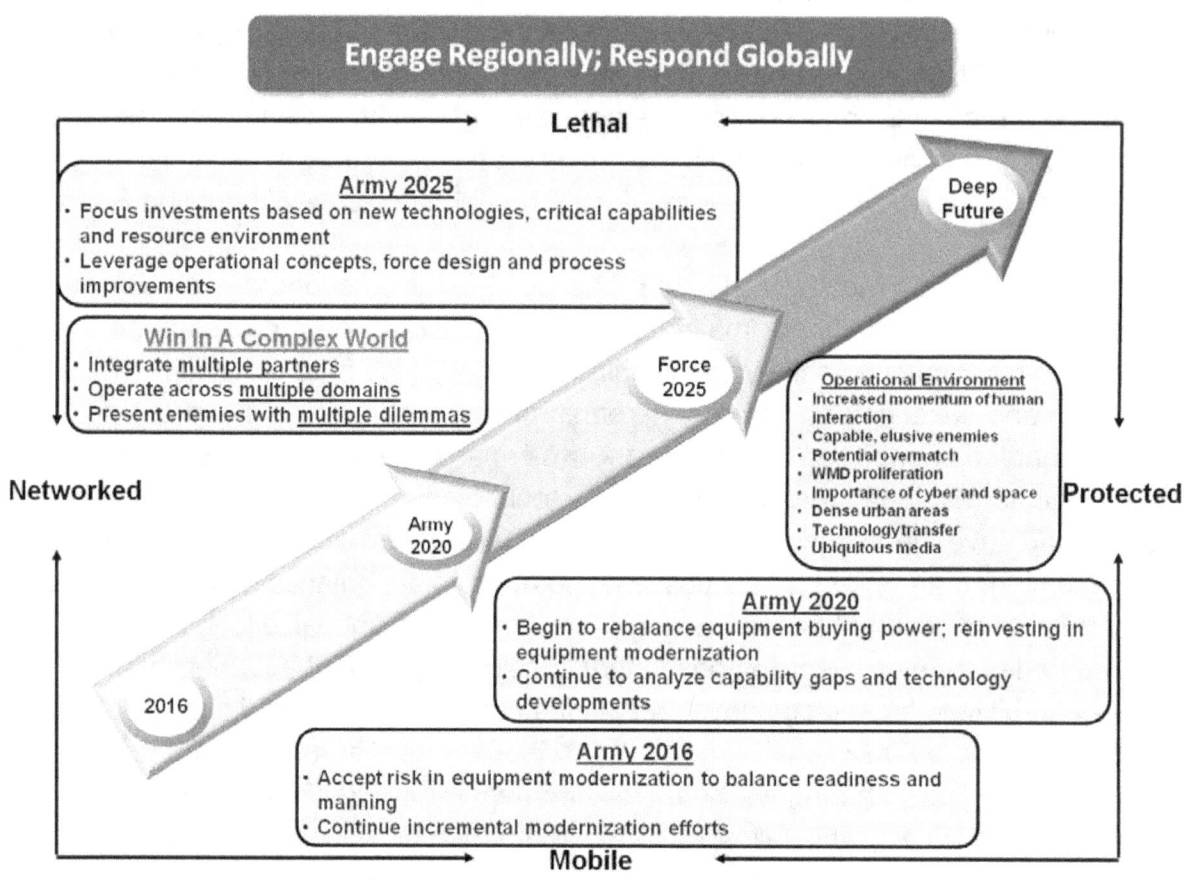

Figure 1. Cornerstone Capabilities

Figure 1 above depicts the cornerstone capabilities required to build discriminately lethal squads and small units. Our strategic intent is to modernize and equip the Total Army with equipment that is affordable, sustainable, and cost-effective to provide ready and tailorable land power supporting the full range of combatant command requirements. To achieve these strategic priorities the Army will focus on the following:

- Prioritize Soldier-centered modernization and procurement of proven technologies so that Soldiers have the best weapons, equipment and protection to accomplish every mission.
- Seek fundamental improvements to Soldier and unit system lethality, survivability, mobility, and network functionality to ensure that the American Soldier remains the most discriminately lethal force on the battlefield.
- Focus Science and Technology investment to maximize the potential of emerging game-changing land power technologies to counter emerging threats and to ensure that Army formations retain a decisive materiel edge and tactical overmatch across the range of military operations. Additionally, the Army must maintain the ability to conduct the range of operations in a Global Positioning System (GPS) denied environment.
- Ensure that Army units are prepared for new, emerging, and evolving missions in areas such as space, cyberspace, missile defense, and countering weapons of mass destruction.
- Equip the Total Army to rapidly deploy, fight, sustain itself, and win against complex state and non-state threats in austere environments and rugged terrain (the expeditionary mindset).

Resource Linkage: *Versatile and Tailorable, yet Affordable and Cost-Effective*

The Army goal is to develop and field the mix of equipment needed to ensure that our Soldiers have the right equipment, for the right missions, at the right time. However, the Army is accepting risk by temporarily curtailing equipment modernization efforts to balance unit readiness until we complete force structure reductions allowing us to restore resources to reestablish our modernization tempo. The Army's core capability rests in its Soldiers. Rather than acquire equipment first, then man those systems, the Army organizes its Soldiers first, then trains and equips them to prevail against the challenges they will face. For example, an important partner is the Army's Human-Systems Integration (HSI) office, whose core mission is milestone assessment of developing systems to fit the equipment to the Soldier, not the Soldier to the equipment.

The Army has an established framework, as depicted in Figure 2, to guide equipment modernization. The strategy focuses our efforts on the Soldier and squad as the foundation of our Army. This means building from the Soldier out and equipping our squads for tactical overmatch in all situations by ensuring they are connected to an integrated network and that they are in vehicles that are survivable, mobile and lethal.

Modernization Strategy in a Fiscally Challenged Environment

- Reduce procurement quantities to match force structure reductions
- Gained efficiencies
  - Leveraging multi-year procurement
  - Incorporate Better Buying Power initiatives (contracting, should-cost, competition)

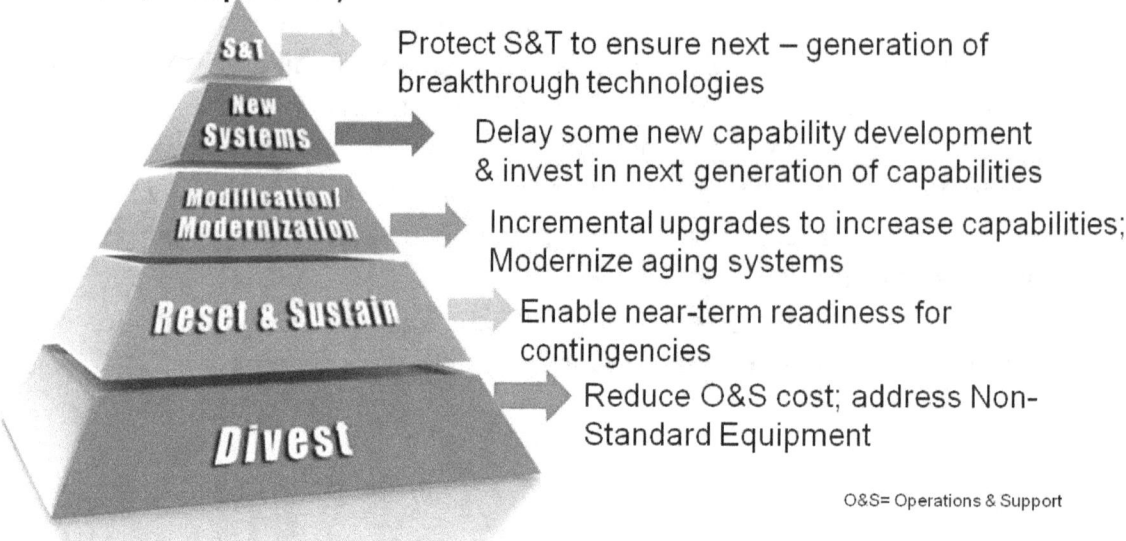

S&T → Protect S&T to ensure next – generation of breakthrough technologies

New Systems → Delay some new capability development & invest in next generation of capabilities

Modification Modernization → Incremental upgrades to increase capabilities; Modernize aging systems

Reset & Sustain → Enable near-term readiness for contingencies

Divest → Reduce O&S cost; address Non-Standard Equipment

O&S= Operations & Support

Figure 2. Army Modernization Framework

The tiers of a modernization strategy begin with protecting S&T to ensure the next generation of breakthrough technologies is available to apply to equipment designs. So far the Army has been successful at maintaining S&T funding levels even while reducing the RDA budget. The Army will continue analysis of War Fighting Challenges to focus and apply technology advances to current and future capabilities.

Next, the Army must delay some new capability developments and invest in next generation capabilities based on operational value, capabilities shortfalls, and available resources. As described in last year's plan the Army did not transition critical modernization programs such as Ground Combat Vehicle or Armed Aerial Scout. Since 2011, the Army has ended 20 programs, delayed 125 and restructured 124. These program decisions were directly linked to constrained resource levels and indicate the extent of reduced modernization efforts with available Army resources.

Without a range of new systems to replace aging systems the Army must improve its existing systems with incremental upgrades. These upgrades improve capabilities; reduce size, weight and power requirements; reduce complexity to the Soldier; improve operational energy usage and improve safety. Additionally, this continuous improvement of existing systems helps to sustain the industrial base and organic engineering skills.

Army program reductions have limited the Army's ability to reset and repair equipment returning from Afghanistan. This returning equipment is critical to rebuilding unit readiness to stay prepared for near-term contingency operations. The Army will require supplemental funding for three years, even after our combat involvement in Afghanistan is complete, to reset our equipment from the harsh demands of war. This continued reset will also assist in maintaining important capabilities in the Army's organic industrial base.

Finally, the Army must aggressively divest of equipment that is obsolete, excess to needs because of declining manpower levels, or not economically feasible to repair. Divestment also reduces operating and sustainment costs. More than 11 years of war led to a proliferation of non-standard equipment. The Army Requirements Oversight Council reviews non-standard systems and determines the actions necessary for retention, disposal or other disposition of this equipment. These decisions help the Army to bridge between current equipping posture and future modernization requirements while addressing sustainment cost concerns.

PB16 Overview and Main Effort (ME):

Decreases to the Army budget over the past several years have had significant impacts on Army modernization and threaten our ability to retain overmatch through the next decade. The Army was able to maintain S&T funding at the FY 2015 levels, but program impacts from FY 2015 carry into FY 2016 causing the Army to assume risk by delaying the development of many new capabilities. Under sequestration, it is estimated there will be over 80 programs affected in FY 2016. Major impacts include delays in equipping to support expeditionary forces, delays in combat vehicle and aviation modernization, increases in sustainment costs to fix older equipment and increases in capability gaps.

Army guidance in developing this budget was to fund critical Soldier enabling capabilities – target acquisition, lethality, protection systems; fully fund all Acquisition Category (ACAT) I programs; fund Aviation Restructure Initiative (ARI) to include modernization of aircraft; fund the 4th Stryker Double V-Hull (DVH) Brigade (with Engineering Change Proposals (ECP)); protect S&T funding at PB15 levels; implement

Network capability review decisions; protect multiyear procurements and procure at or above minimum sustainment rates. This budget meets that guidance.

The majority of the impact of the decrements in the PB 16 budget is to large programs that can absorb the decrement without breaking – allowing the ability to buy back schedule and quantities in the future. Some mitigation efforts include: Slow engineering change proposals for Abrams and Bradley combat vehicles; slow procurement and fielding for Patriot modernization; and adjust Warfighter Information Network – Tactical (WIN-T) fielding quantities.

There are three main efforts this year that characterize equipment modernization. These efforts are:

Focused Technology Investment: The Army intent is to protect core capabilities aligned with the 30-year strategic equipment plans and foster innovation, maturation and demonstration of technology enabling capabilities to prepare for the Army of the future. The Army met Defense Department guidance to fund S&T at PB15 levels. The key efforts are in combat vehicle prototyping, assured Position/Navigation/Timing (PNT) and technology demonstrations for Joint Multi Role helicopter and High Energy Laser efforts. We are also able to continue some investments in technologies for degraded visual environments, long range fires, cyber, high energy laser, materials, and quantum science technologies.

System Development: The Army has limited systems in development and we have slowed the pace of development to meet budget parameters while accepting risk of reduced overmatch for the remainder of this decade. Some systems that this budget continues to support and increase capabilities in the near- and mid-term are:

- Tactical Vehicles: Armored Multipurpose Vehicle and Joint Light Tactical Vehicle;

- Air and Missile Defense: Integrated Battle Command System (IBCS); Indirect Fire Protection Capability (IFPC 2-I); future radar;

- Aviation: Improved Turbine Engine Program (ITEP);

- Intelligence and Electronic Warfare: Maintains Aerial ISR 2020 Strategy; and

- Network: Small Airborne Network Radio (SANR).

System Upgrades and Procurement: By continuing to develop and improve existing components, sub-systems, and systems the Army improves capabilities. Our priority focus is to enhance capabilities of the current force through low risk and cost-effective fleet modernization. Some examples are:

- Soldier Equipment: Maintains our priority focus on Soldiers; fields systems such as Soldier Protection Systems, Counter-Defilade Target Engagement systems, and Family of Weapon Sights;

- Vehicles: Double-V Hull for four of nine Stryker Brigades; HERCULES recovery vehicles for nine of 15 Armored Brigade Combat Teams (ABCT); Paladin upgrade for seven ABCT; Abrams upgrades for two ABCT; Bradley upgrades for four ABCT;

- Aviation: CH-47F for three Chinook companies; AH-64E for two Apache battalions, UH-60M for two Assault battalions and two Medical Evacuation (MEDEVAC) companies; Light Utility Helicopter (LUH) for the training base;

- Integrated Fires and Air Defense: Procures insensitive munitions compliant Alternative Warhead for 63 percent of the Guided Multiple Launch Rocket System (GMLRS) inventory; service life extension for 10 percent of the Army Tactical Missile System (ATACMS) inventory; upgrades to Patriot systems; improved Patriot missile for 17 percent of the missile inventory; and

- Network: Synchronizes network capabilities by procuring WIN-T Increment 2 for three brigades, three division headquarters and six battalions realigned to Brigade Combat Teams (BCT). Procures and fields Handheld, Manpack, and Small Form Fit (HMS) Rifleman Radio systems for three Operational Capability Set BCTs in FY 2016. Additionally, procures Joint Battle Command-Platform (JBC-P) for approximately 30 BCTs and Brigade size formations, including replacement of Enhanced Position Location and Reporting System (EPLRS) radios in BCTs.

Summary:

As lower funding levels for the Army continue, we are concerned about the health of the industrial base and the subsequent consequences for the Army and our Nation. Teaming and collaboration with our industrial base, early in the process, will help reduce risk. This will also ensure that our Army is adequately postured with the necessary skills, facilities, and capabilities to meet future challenges. Shrinking demands for new combat platforms and smaller production rates lead to higher proportional costs. A smaller defense industrial complex may reflect a workforce with reduced design, development, and manufacturing expertise. Diminished capacity in our industrial base may decrease competitiveness and slow response time to future requirements.

Our equipment modernization efforts reflect the priorities of a relatively modern Army with constrained resources. Affordability and cost-effectiveness are prime factors in planning resources to modernize our equipment and close capability gaps in this fiscal environment.

In a perfect world, the Army can ensure that Soldiers have the best equipment through sufficient, predictable and consistent funding. Because of today's fiscal uncertainty and constrained budgets, the Army has decided to take risk in modernization. Equipment modernization risk is defined as the decline in technical overmatch of equipment against an enemy's capabilities. When sequestration-level budget caps return this year, the research, development and acquisition accounts will bear the burden of the unrelenting reductions. Accordingly this will directly impact every modernization priority and over 80 acquisition programs in FY 2016 are vulnerable, particularly the large ones.

Army Fiscal Year 2016 Budget Objectives and Critical Programs

Over the past four years, the Army has absorbed several budgetary reductions in the midst of conducting operations overseas and rebalancing the force to the wider array of missions called for in the 2012 Defense Strategy Guidance. Overall, Research, Development and Acquisition funding is reduced and the long term effect will be additional stress on current fleets, reduced replacement of war worn equipment, challenges sustaining the industrial base and modernization of only the most critical capabilities.

The Army focuses on effectively using constrained resources for near-term requirements and tailoring our long-term investments to provide the right capabilities for Soldiers in the future. This approach calls for carefully planned investment strategies across all Army equipment portfolios, which will involve a mix of limiting the development of new capabilities, incrementally upgrading existing platforms and investing in key technologies to support future modernization efforts. The Army has established overarching equipment budget priorities and objectives to help guide our investment strategies, as described below.

While no one can accurately predict one hundred percent of the Army's long-term future fiscal resources, a credible baseline funding projection is a key element to determining the affordability of acquisition programs. Along with an improved approach in transitioning the Program Objective Memorandum (POM) data into budget data, Army leaders now have a higher level of confidence in the continuity and consistency of budget, programming and long-range financial planning data. This was largely made possible by the Long-range Investment Requirements Analysis (LIRA) process which allows for better planning and forecasting--a more realistic and effective investment strategy—needed today due to shrinking resources, constrained budget and pressing fiscal challenges facing the federal government.

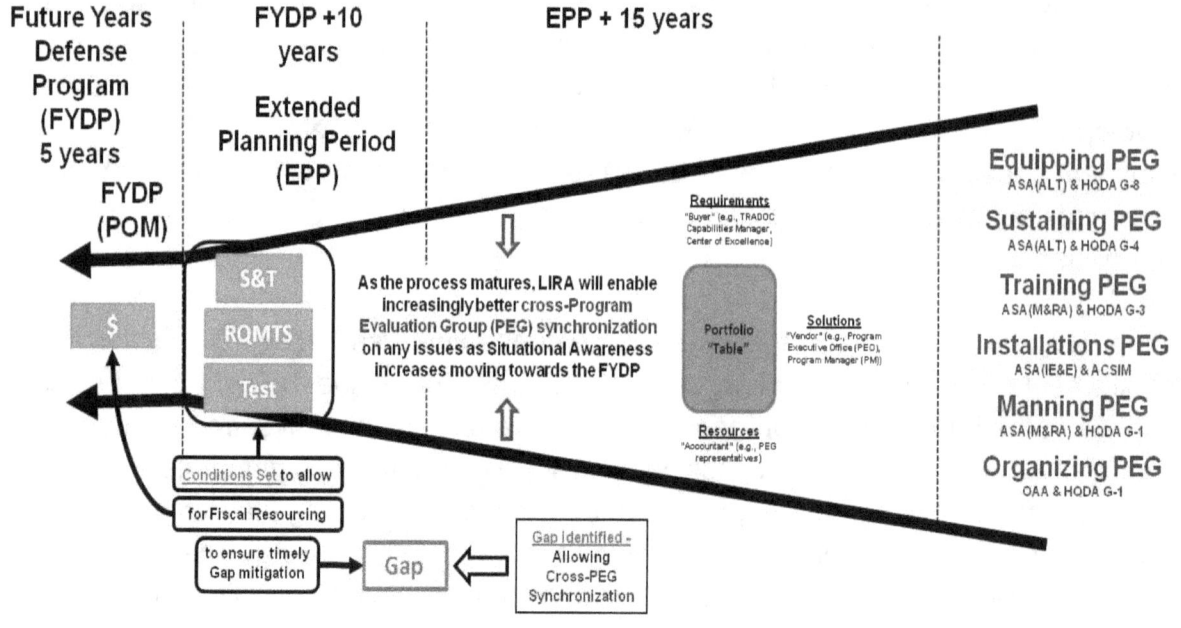

Figure 3. LIRA Process

As depicted in Figure 3, LIRA annually examines the life-cycle affordability of estimated future materiel requirements over a 30-year period against its estimated total obligation authority or legal spending limit. There are six Program Executive Groups (PEG) that align with the Title 10 responsibilities of the Secretary of the Army and LIRA uses four: Training, Equipping, Sustaining and Installation. The collaborative process established in LIRA allows Army stakeholders the opportunity to de-conflict long-term planning for an existing or future capability.

Now that the Army Operating Concept and companion Force 2025 and Beyond implementation are emerging it will be critical to match Warfighting Challenges solutions with the available resources to continue to equip Soldiers with the best available equipment.

Equipment Budget Priorities and Objectives

- **Enhance the Soldier for Broad Joint Mission Support.**

The centerpiece of the Army's Modernization Strategy continues to be the Soldier and the Squad. The Army's objective is to facilitate incremental improvements by rapidly integrating technologies and applications that empower, protect, and unburden the Soldier and our formations, thus providing the Soldier and our formations with the mobility, protection, situational awareness and lethality to accomplish assigned missions. The FY 2016 budget supports this priority by investing in technologies that provide the Soldier and squad improvements in enhanced weapon effects, next generation optics and night vision devices, advanced body armor and individual protection equipment, unmanned aerial systems, ground based robots, and Soldier power systems.

- **Enable Mission Command.**

The Army's objective is to facilitate the decision-making of leaders and Soldiers with information to the point of need across the Joint Force down to the Soldier and across platforms with a goal of agile and expeditionary tactical command posts supported by robust home station architecture. The FY 2016 budget supports this priority by resourcing enhanced mission command capabilities and platform integration of network components through Operational Capability Sets, software applications for the Common Operating Environment, operations/intelligence network convergence efforts and platform integration of network components in support of Operational Capability Sets.

- **Remain Prepared for Joint Combined Arms Maneuver.**

The Army's objective is to facilitate fleet capabilities to increase lethality and mobility while optimizing protection by managing the full suite of capabilities to enable the most stressing joint war fights. The FY 2016 budget supports this priority by resourcing the Armored Multi-Purpose Vehicle, Paladin Integrated Management program, Joint Light Tactical Vehicle and critical Aviation programs.

The Army has identified critical programs that provide the Army the top-line capabilities in a stressing joint war fight. These systems provide the Army overmatch capabilities at the tactical and operational levels of combat operations. These critical programs are:

- **Warfighter Information Network-Tactical (WIN-T) ($43.5M Research, Development, Test and Evaluation (RDTE) / $783.1M Other Procurement, Army (OPA) / $20.8M Operations and Maintenance, Army (OMA))** provides the broadband backbone communications necessary for the tactical Army. It extends an Internet Protocol based satellite and line-of-sight communications network through the tactical force supporting voice, data and video.

- **Family of Networked Tactical Radios ($31.6M RDTE / $92.4M OPA)** is the Army's future deployable mobile communications family of radio systems; including Handheld, Manpack, and Small Form Fit radios, Mid-Tier Wideband Networking Vehicular radios and Small Airborne Networking radios; providing advanced joint tactical end-to-end networking data and voice communications to mounted platforms, dismounted troops and aircraft platforms.

- **Joint Battle Command-Platform (JBC-P) ($2.7M RDTE / $133.3M OPA)** is the next generation of Force XXI Battle Command Brigade and Below / Blue Force Tracking and is the foundation for achieving affordable information interoperability and superiority on current and future battlefields and is the principal command and control / situation awareness (C2 / SA) system for the Army and Marine Corps at the brigade level and-below.

- **Distributed Common Ground System-Army (DCGS-A) ($25.6M RDTE / $260.3M OPA)** provides integrated Intelligence, Surveillance, Reconnaissance (ISR) Processing, Exploitation and Dissemination of airborne and ground sensor data, providing commanders at all levels, access to the Defense Intelligence Information Enterprise and leverages the entire national, joint, tactical and coalition ISR community.

- **Nett Warrior ($12.4M RDTE / $49.8M OPA)** is a dismounted Soldier worn mission command system providing unprecedented C2 / SA capabilities supporting the dismounted combat leader. The design incorporates operational unit mission needs and leverages operational lessons learned, while maintaining power requirements in austere environments.

- **Armored Multi-Purpose Vehicle (AMPV) ($230.2M RDTE)** replaces the M113 family of vehicles within the ABCTs and provides required protection, mobility and networking capability for the Army's critical enablers including mortars, medical evacuation, medical treatment, general purpose as well as mission command vehicles.

- **Patriot ($172.2M RDTE / $804.6M MSLS)** is a high demand / low density program, currently deployed in multiple theaters supporting operational and strategic requirements. Patriot provides critical, sustained, tactical ballistic missile defense capability to defeat current and advanced threats while protecting Soldiers, sailors, airmen and marines.

- **Paladin Integrated Management (PIM) ($152.3M RDTE / $273.9M WTCV)** replaces the current M109A6 Paladin and M992A2 Field Artillery Ammunition Supply Vehicle with a more robust platform incorporating Bradley common drive train and suspension components in a newly designed hull.

- **Joint Light Tactical Vehicle (JLTV) ($32.5M RDTE / $308.3M OPA)** is the centerpiece of the Army's Tactical Wheeled Vehicle modernization strategy replacing 49,099 of the light wheeled vehicle fleet by 2041. Providing enhanced protection for Soldiers, this multi-mission vehicle will provide sustained and networked mobility for personnel and payloads across the full range of military operations whether traditional or irregular.

- **Maneuver Support Vessel – Light (MSV-L) ($10.1M RDTE)** represents a modernization of current Army watercraft capabilities provided by the aging Vietnam War era Landing Craft Mechanized 8 Mod I and II (LCM-8). The MSV-L adds new capabilities intended to meet the Army's future tactical and operational movement and maneuver requirements. MSV-L is intended to access austere entry points, degraded ports, and bare beaches without dependency on support ashore, in support of land maneuver support and / or maneuver sustainment operations.

- **AH-64 Apache ($69.9M RDTE / $1.49B Procurement, Aircraft (ACFT)** is the Army's world class heavy attack helicopter for the current and future force, assigned to Attack Helicopter Battalions and Armed Reconnaissance Squadrons. The AH-64E provides the capability to conduct simultaneously close combat, mobile strike, armed reconnaissance, security, and vertical maneuver missions across the full spectrum of warfare, whether required in day, night, obscured battlefield or adverse weather conditions.

- **UH-60 Black Hawk ($117.8M RDTE[4] / $1.62B ACFT)** is a utility aircraft and the Army's largest helicopter fleet. The Black Hawk is vital in supporting lift and medical evacuation missions in the current and future force operational plans. The Black Hawk is critical to the homeland defense mission and is a key component of the Army National Guard's forest fire, tornado, hurricane and earthquake relief missions.

---

[4] Includes $51.2M RDTE for Improved Turbine Engine Program

Science and Technology Program

The mission of Army Science & Technology (S&T) is to identify, develop and demonstrate technology options that inform and enable effective and affordable capabilities for the Soldier. The Army S&T program balances investments between "revolutionary" and "evolutionary" research to improve performance of existing warfighting systems and provide new capabilities. The Army S&T program is guided by and aligned to higher level Army, DoD and National strategies and policies and is informed by both current and emerging threats. In addition, the Army identified enduring capability challenges that are necessary to conduct future operations to prevent, shape, and win conflicts, and are used to frame Army modernization. The enduring capability challenges align to the Training and Doctrine Command's (TRADOC) Army Warfighting Challenges and subsequently prioritized to TRADOC Capability Need Analysis gaps which provides a focus for Army S&T investment. Army S&T investments are also aligned to Programs of Record (PoR) through the LIRA process.

For FY 2016, the Army will maintain the 2015 President's Budget level of S&T funding and will sustain or increase resources supporting the Office of the Secretary of Defense (OSD) priority S&T areas (Cyber Operations, Electronic Warfare/Electronic Protection, Data to Decisions, Engineered Resilient Systems, Autonomy, and Human Systems). In FY 2016, the Army has dedicated more than $2B to its S&T Program, all of which is aligned with the Army's needs and priorities: $425M in Research, Development, Test and Evaluation (RDT&E) Budget Activity (BA) 1 (Basic Research), $880M in RDT&E BA 2 (Applied Research), $896M in RDT&E BA 3 (Advanced Technology Demonstrations); $41M in the Technology Maturation Initiatives Program in RDT&E BA 4 (Advanced Component Development and Prototypes); and $48M in the Manufacturing Technology Program in RDT&E BA 7 (Operational System Development).

The Army S&T program is organized into eight investment portfolios that address challenges across six Army-wide capability areas (Soldier/Squad; Air; Ground Maneuver; Command, Control, Communications, and Intelligence (C3I); Lethality; and Medical) and two S&T enabling areas (Basic Research and Innovation Enablers). The following are examples of major thrust areas within the S&T Portfolio:

- The Joint Multi-Role Technology Demonstrator (JMR TD) effort, the foundation for the Army's Future Vertical Lift (FVL) acquisition program, is exploring rotor systems, drives, propulsion systems, structures, platform configurations, mission systems architectures and other associated technologies to support the FVL strategy. Four JMR TD Air Vehicle Technology Investment Agreements were awarded in FY 2013. In early FY 2015, two JMR TD vendors were selected to complete their flight demonstrator designs with the goal of executing flight tests in FY 2017. These flight tests will demonstrate technology options that meet future capability needs and drive down risk for the future PoR.

- The Modular Active Protection System (MAPS) program, initiated in FY 2015, is developing technologies to increase vehicle survivability and protection against current and emerging advanced threats. Technologies developed will provide increased protection while maintaining or reducing vehicle weight by reducing reliance on armor through the use of other means such as sensing, warning, hostile fire detection and active countermeasures. The MAPS effort is a departure from previous active protection system (APS) efforts in that it establishes an APS Common Architecture applicable across all military vehicles. The overall goal of the effort is to demonstrate component capability and validate architecture design to ease integration and facilitate fielding of APS on Army platforms across the ground vehicle fleet. This effort will conclude in FY 2019.

- Army S&T is developing technologies to provide Soldiers the capability to attain trusted Position, Navigation and Timing (PNT) information while operating in conditions that impede or deny access to the Global Positioning System (GPS) with planned transition to the Army's Assured PNT (A-PNT) PoR. These technologies include anti-jam GPS antennas and pseudolite transceivers (an alternative source of GPS-like signals) for transition to A-PNT in FY 2016. In FY 2017, Army S&T will transition A-PNT solutions for mounted and dismounted applications to the A-PNT PoR. Both the mounted and dismounted efforts are structured to provide a hub capability that delivers a position and timing signal to all vehicles or Soldier systems that require PNT.

- Operation in Degraded Visual Environments (DVE) is the leading contributor to helicopter accidents and reduced operational effectiveness. The Army S&T DVE Mitigation Program (DVE-MP) develops a combination of flight control systems, sensors and cueing (2D and 3D symbology, aural and tactile methodologies) to relay critical aircraft and environmental information to the pilot to mitigate mission impacts related to operating in DVE. In FY 2015, tests were conducted on sensors that address brown-out conditions. Future FY 2020 DVE-MP flight tests will demonstrate advanced flight controls, sensor suites, and cockpit cueing to enable 360 degree situational awareness in multiple degraded visual environments.

- Cyber S&T efforts are aligned to operational gaps identified in the cyber capability based assessment, TRADOC emerging doctrine and requirements and the Army Cyber Materiel Development Strategy. Near-term defensive efforts focus on protection technologies that enhance resiliency, trust, and agility of tactical networks and information as well as addressing top tier threat actors. Near-term offensive efforts focus on technologies that provide robust and scalable architectures and cyber geo-location. In FY 2016, S&T will integrate software with the Army Brigade network to provide holistic cyber situational awareness for assurance teams to assess the cyber battle space, detect/defend against known cyber weapons and enable network adaptation.

- Electronic Warfare (EW) S&T efforts focus on designing countermeasures to address threats against Army helicopter, ground mounted platforms and dismounted Soldiers. In addition, Army S&T is developing architectures to deconflict sensing and response between EW and cyber assets in the battlespace. In FY 2016, S&T will demonstrate EW techniques and effects against target threat unmanned aerial systems and will integrate signals intelligence and cyber detection/response capabilities into a common chassis utilizing a set of standards-based open modular architectures to improve capability and interoperability.

- The Combat Vehicle Prototyping (CVP) Program, initiated in FY 2015, matures technologies to address technical and integration challenges facing the ground combat fleet in the areas of mobility, protection, lethality, and vehicle architecture. CVP focuses on maturation and demonstration of technologies such as engines, transmissions, integrated starter generators, ballistic protection, blast mitigation, advanced material technologies, lethality subsystems and advanced fire controls. The goal is to mature and demonstrate by FY 2019 a series of subsystem demonstrators that will inform the requirements for the future fighting vehicle (FFV), identify insertion opportunities for the legacy ground platform fleet, and drive down future PoR risk.

- Prototyping has become an area of increased emphasis across the Department of Defense and is reflected in our increased funding towards developing demonstrators such as JMR TD and CVP. Building prototypes early in the lifecycle of proposed systems gives the Army (and Soldiers) a better idea of what the system looks, feels, and performs like; affords an opportunity to try out innovative approaches prior to committing to a major PoR for a technology; and helps to drive down considerable program risk as we work through those unanticipated integration issues. Experimentation adds another layer of benefit. By putting technology into the hands of the Warfighter, we learn practical insights, identify human factors issues early and expose Soldiers to new innovative technology in a non-threatening but relevant operational environment. The Army's BA 4 funding (Technology Maturation Initiative) was established to facilitate this pre-PoR activity. This BA4 activity is designed to reduce the PoR acquisition timeline through early S&T prototype work that is used to help define achievable and affordable requirements, ultimately driving down program risks. The benefit of using prototypes can be illustrated by the Future Tactical Truck System (FTTS) S&T program which designed and developed three drivable prototype systems that emphasized the use of innovative technology and afforded Soldiers and the Army the ability to try out these technologies / capabilities before they finalized the requirements for the Joint Light Tactical Vehicle (JLTV).

- Vulnerability assessments, another key component of the S&T strategy, require an increased collaboration with the intelligence community to ensure we understand the threat that exists and the potential threat of the future. The intent is to challenge assumptions regarding technology and system employment in an operational environment that may lead to unforeseen risks in acquiring new systems. Assessment outcomes are intended to provide timely feedback to technology and materiel developers, increasing awareness of potential technology vulnerabilities and identifying tradeoffs or opportunities for design improvements that may not have been considered. This effort will also seek to uncover potential "enterprise" vulnerabilities, such as impacts in systems-of-systems integration, training, logistics and Warfighter adaptability. Ultimately, these activities aim to preclude the introduction of unforeseen risks and vulnerabilities as new technologies are adopted by the Army and promote the development of S&T products that are "threat ready."

- In Basic Research in FY 2016, an emerging focus area is Quantum Effects where Army S&T is pursuing the exploitation of unique quantum properties to design viable mobile and secure quantum networks, enable ultra-precise sensors and imaging through the use of quantum effects. Research investigations include: developing hybrid quantum systems; developing quantum nodes, novel interfaces and memory; theoretical models of protocols and algorithms for distributed quantum network platforms; and, developments of quantum systems as quantum simulators. For the Army, techniques like entangled photon key distribution and information teleportation have an impact that is pervasive and profound, including: enhanced, jam-proof position and navigation; quantum computing; advanced and novel sensing; and secure communications. The expected payoff is anywhere from 5 – 50 years depending on which research topic area is under discussion.

These aforementioned efforts are important as the Army faces an extended funding downturn over the next five years resulting in fewer transition opportunities. The resultant pause in acquisition provides an opportunity to invest in innovative, potentially disruptive research that doesn't have an immediate PoR transition opportunity. By prototyping the most promising innovative technologies, we not only demonstrate their potential payoff, but we keep Army expertise focused on developing affordable and achievable capabilities and informing our long-range planning process to identify future transition opportunities. During this time, the S&T community will serve an important role in preparing to capitalize on S&T investments once the Army emerges from reduced acquisition funding near the end of the decade. Army S&T will target critical technology areas and future acquisition programs, such as assured position, navigation and timing, the next generation combat vehicle, the next-generation helicopter and affordable active protection systems.

As the Army S&T Program continues to identify and harvest technologies suitable for transition to our force, we aim to remain ever vigilant of potential and emerging threats. We are implementing a strategic approach to modernization that includes an awareness of existing and potential gaps; an understanding of emerging threats; knowledge of state-of-the-art commercial, academic, and government research; as well as a clear understanding of competing needs for limited resources. Army S&T will sharpen its research efforts to focus upon those core capabilities it needs to sustain while identifying promising or disruptive technologies. Ultimately, the focus remains upon Soldiers; Army S&T consistently seeks new avenues to increase the Soldier's capability and ensure their technological superiority today, tomorrow, and decades from now.

Conclusion

"And while we've been focused on fighting insurgency in two places and terrorism world-wide, the world has not stood still. Our friends and enemies have not stood still. And technology has not stood still. And so this for us is a time to look up, look around, and look forward at what the world will need from us next – to the security challenges that will define our future after Iraq and Afghanistan."[5]

The security challenges of tomorrow will be met with the equipment we are developing, modernizing, and procuring today. Because adversaries will continue to invest in technology to counter or evade U.S. strengths, resource reductions and insufficient force modernization place at risk the Army's ability to overmatch its opponents. Joint and Army forces may not have ready units in sufficient scale to respond to and resolve all the world's crises due to decreasing budgets.

The Army hasn't had a budget approved in place, on time, since FY 2007. Congress has enacted 16 continuing resolutions since FY 2010. Continuing resolutions hamper and delay critical programs; prevent us from reprogramming money to make smart choices with limited funds; and stop new starts to fill current and emerging requirements. Even with the addition of the Bi-Partisan Budget Act funding in FY 2014 and FY 2015, only a third (34 percent) of our brigade combat teams are fully trained to conduct unified land operations. Operation United Assistance (Ebola Support) will require continued Overseas Humanitarian Disaster Assistance, and Civic Aid funding ($1B is reprogrammed from FY 2014 and waiting Congressional approval for FY 2015). Operation Inherent Resolve is paid for primarily out of Overseas Contingency Operations funds and the Army is seeking Security Assistance funding to train vetted friendly elements. Operations in east Europe are funded out of Base programs. The Army needs support for the European Reassurance Initiative (ERI) with $1B in FY 2015 and continued support in FY 2016. The Army needs new base closure and realignments, approval of proposed compensation reforms, and our Aviation Restructure Initiative; without them we will be forced to make further cuts to readiness, end strength, and modernization. With Congressional support for the Army's proposed reforms and initiatives and manning authorization for a 980K total force the Army will be able to meet its National defense requirements.

The Army must continue to emphasize long-range planning, making sure that acquisition decisions account for the full life cycle costs of the equipment. We must continue to incrementally modernize our existing equipment and plan for future developments when balance to the Army budget is restored. The Army is focusing investment for new technologies across portfolios to enable capabilities that will optimize Soldier performance, enhance maneuverability and increase lethality. S&T

---

[5] Ashton B. Carter, Deputy Secretary of Defense, Remarks at the Woodrow Wilson Center, October 03, 2012

investments must be protected to prepare for the future and allow for the innovation of future solutions. Few choices remain if modernization accounts must bear the brunt of sequestration. Most programs are already at minimum economic sustaining levels and further reductions will rapidly increase the number of cancellations. Those programs remaining will have high unit costs and be significantly extended in time. This severely reduces buying power, further delays filling capability gaps and forces the Army to tier modernization. Rapid regeneration of equipment to fill modernization gaps comes at a premium in cost and time.

SOLDIER

Section I. Overview

The squad is the foundation of the decisive force and the cornerstone of all Army units. The Soldier Portfolio focuses on equipping the individual Soldier and squad to maintain overmatch on the battlefield in terms of lethality, situational awareness, protection, and mobility. Soldier and squad equipment and weapons include: individual and crew-served weapons, shoulder-fired and vehicle-mounted close combat missiles, mortars, Soldier sensors and lasers, night vision devices, body armor, Soldier clothing, individual equipment, parachutes, limited tactical communications equipment and unmanned ground systems (see figure 4). Operational overmatch provides Soldiers with a combined arms capability to effectively detect, recognize, acquire, engage and neutralize or destroy targets at all ranges.

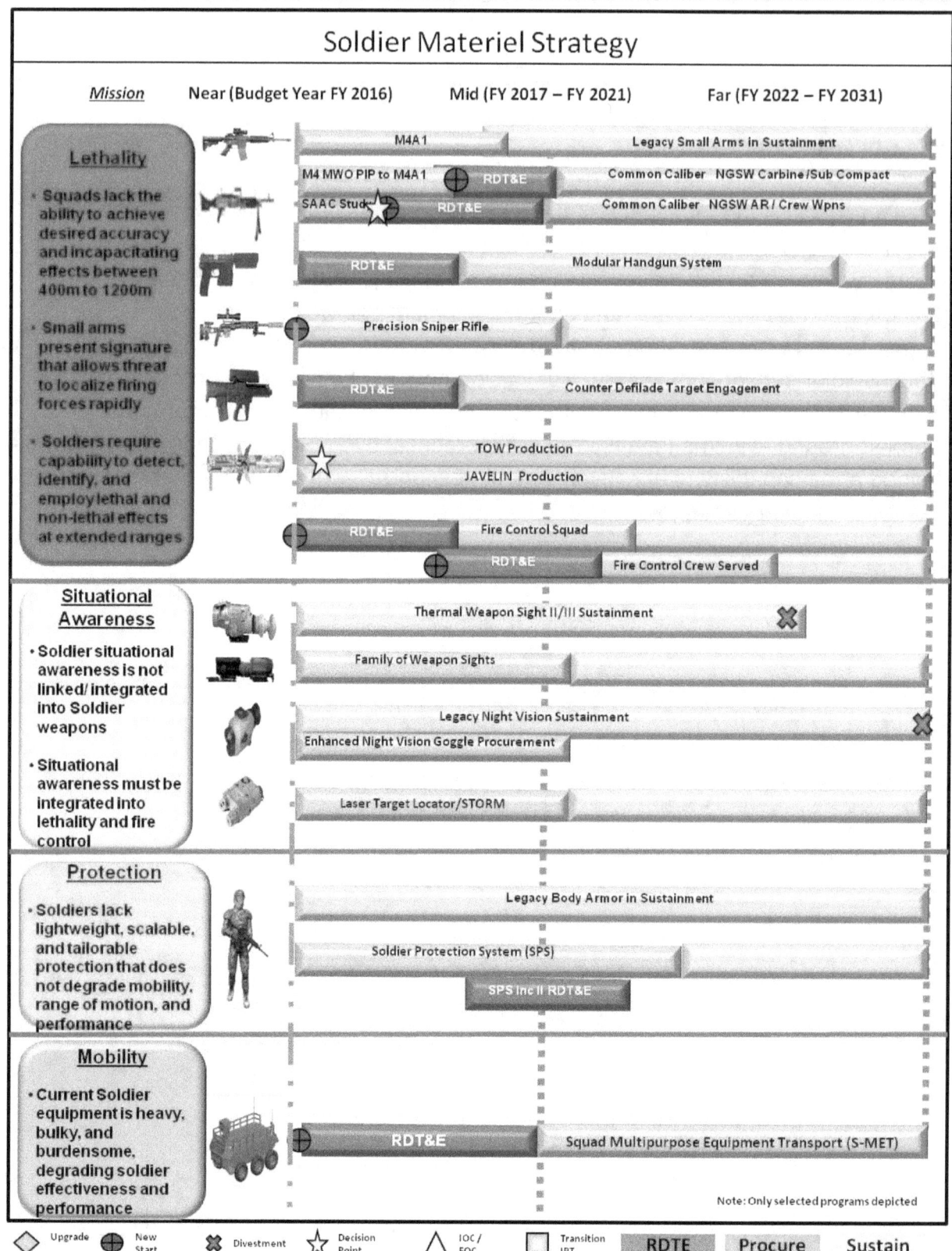

Figure 4. Soldier (See acronym glossary)

Section II. Strategy Update

To meet the readiness and modernization objectives of The Army Plan, the Soldier and Squad portfolio objectives for FY 2016 are:

- Conduct a small arms caliber and configuration study to inform next generation small arms modernization decisions.
- Support the extended Engineering and Manufacturing Development (EMD) phase of the XM-25, Counter Defilade Target Engagement System which is the next step in employing this revolutionary Soldier-level precision weapon system. The intent of extending the EMD phase is to improve system lethality and incorporate Engineering Change Proposal (ECP) changes to the target acquisition/fire control capability.
- Continue the fielding of Enhanced Night Vision Devices to deploying Special Operation Forces (SOF) and BCTs.
- Continue replacement of the conventional force parachute inventory with the Advanced Tactical Parachute System.
- Continue to improve Soldier/Squad mobility and load reduction efforts through research and development in body armor, weapons and selected energy solutions to extend dismounted Soldiers' range and endurance.
- Expand the development of unmanned ground systems (UGS) to provide Squad and Platoon remote reconnaissance with the Common Robotic System – Individual (CRS-I) and reduced Soldier workload for mobility and sustainment with the Squad Multipurpose Equipment Transport (SMET).
- Significantly improve the storage, generation, and management of tactical Soldier and Squad power with the Small Unit Power program.
- Provide the Fire Resistant Environmental Ensemble to aircrews improving their protection and comfort.

Section III. Key Soldier and Squad Portfolio Accomplishments (FY 2014 / 2015)

- Reduced Soldier load in Afghanistan by replacing Generation III Improved Outer Tactical Vests with Soldier Plate Carrier System (10.5 pounds). Additionally, the weight of the 81mm Mortar was reduced by 20 pounds and the 60mm Mortar was reduced by 8.8 pounds.
- Provided Soldiers with the best possible carbine by procuring improved M4A1s (rather than M4 Carbines), redesigned magazines, and converting existing M4 Carbines into improved M4A1s. Capability improvements include a heavier barrel for greater barrel life, fully automatic trigger and selector switch, ambidextrous

controls, improved sustained rate of fire, a consistent trigger pull and improved ergonomics and handling characteristics.

- Continued procuring the following small arms weapon initiatives with:
  - ➤ 50,829 M4A1 Carbines from new production to support the Army "pure fleet" strategy (replacing M16 family), while converting 65,311 M4s to M4A1s through Product Improvement Program (PIP) Modification Work Orders (MWOs).
  - ➤ 1,658 kits to convert .50 caliber machine guns to enhanced .50 caliber Heavy Machine Gun (HMG) to eliminate the need to set head space and timing.
- Limited procurement and increased research and development of Soldier night vision equipment for current and future contingencies enhancing Soldier lethality and situational awareness across the full range of missions:
  - ➤ 587 Laser Target Locators for BCTs.
  - ➤ 973 Small Tactical Optical Rifle-Mounted (STORM) (micro laser range finders) for dismounted infantry and scouts in BCTs.
  - ➤ 1420 Enhanced Night Vision Goggles for BCTs.

Section IV. Key FY 2016 Soldier and Squad Portfolio Investments

The FY 2016 Soldier investments total $1.1B ($183.0M Weapons and Tracked Combat Vehicles (WTCV) / $218.1M Research, Development, Test and Evaluation (RDTE) / $387M Other Procurement, Army (OPA) / $184.3M Missile Procurement, Army (MSLS) / $122.9M Operation & Maintenance, Army (OMA) / $3.2M Procurement, Ammunition (AMMO)). Includes small arms (individual and crew-served weapons), night vision, Soldier sensors, body armor, Soldier clothing and individual equipment and parachutes. Specific investments in this portfolio include:

- $98.0M (OPA) procures 6095 Enhanced Night Vision Goggles for Brigade Combat Teams.
- $62.0M (WTCV) continues small arms investment which procures 43,074 M4A1 procurement which supports the Army "pure fleet strategy (replacing M16 family); converts 95,003 M4s to M4A1s via PIP MWOs; and procures carbine accessories (Close Quarters Battle Kits, cleaning kits and redesigned magazines). The M4A1 provides Soldiers with close quarter capability at extended ranges with accurate lethal fire.
- $26.2M (OPA) procures 580 Laser Target Locators.
- $23.2M (OPA) procures 2,547 STORM (micro laser range finders).
- $26.0M [6] (OPA) fields new personnel parachutes and accessories for three BCTs and SOF units.

---

[6] Funding amount only for personnel parachutes; cargo parachutes addressed in Sustainment (Service Support) Portfolio.

- $26.3M (WTCV) to buy 8,297 M320A1 40MM Grenade Launchers.
- $8.4M (WTCV) for Common Remotely Operated Weapon Station (CROWS) supports upgrades to existing systems, fielding and training.
- $43.6M (OPA) to procure 40,798 Small Unit Power sets including: Integrated Soldier Power/Data Systems, conformal wearable batteries, and Squad Power Managers.
- $34.4M (RDTE) to complete the development of the CRS-I with a Universal Controller.
- $5.9M (RDTE) in the Robotics Enhancement Program (REP) to support the Army's buy-try-decide methodology for non-developmental robotic systems.

MISSION COMMAND

Section I. Overview

The Mission Command Network will provide expeditionary, uninterrupted mission command through a network comprised of intuitive, secured, standards-based capabilities adapted to commander's requirements and integrated into a common operating environment. Network capabilities will be assured, interoperable, tailorable, collaborative, identity-based, and accessible at the point of need in operations that include unified action partners. This portfolio consists of four capability areas: Transport, Common Operating Environment (COE) / Applications, Support to Cyber Operations, Enablers and Supporting Programs. The primary Transport programs are Warfighter Information Network – Tactical (WIN-T), Nett Warrior and the Family of Networked Tactical Radios. The key Application programs are Tactical Mission Command (TMC), Joint Battle Command – Platform (JBC-P), Global Combat Support System – Army (GCSS-Army) and migration to the COE. The key Network support to cyber programs are Communication Security with Key Management Infrastructure, Information Systems and Security Program and Assured Position Navigation Timing (A-PNT). The key enabler programs are Power Generation and Environmental Control Units (ECU). The Network Integration Evaluation (NIE) is the principal integration effort to enable focused testing, integration, and demonstrations.

As depicted in figures 5 and 6 below, the end state is a coherent, intuitive network of sensors, Soldiers, platforms and command posts linked by a robust transport network with an enabling suite of command and control applications and the necessary Network Operations (NetOps) tools providing our Soldiers a resilient and rapidly configurable network. Key characteristics of the objective network are: scalability and expeditionary with intuitive user interfaces and ease of use; effective Unit Task Reorganization (UTR); fully integrated horizontally and vertically across formations; and a single converged transport across all functional capabilities.

The COE remains an Army priority effort that will significantly improve how we develop, procure, field, update and integrate software for the Soldier. The COE is a set of computing standards, software components and technologies that enable simplified mission command, reduces duplicative applications and shortens the development/test/field time cycle. It implements a software infrastructure akin to smart phone and tablet apps for use in the command post, mounted and handheld environments. Successful COE development has the potential to provide the Army with a leap ahead in how we provide network security and how the Army ultimately achieves simplification of the network and mission command.

The network supports both the operating and generating force, shares information across levels of classification and with the implementation of the COE, enables efficiencies, effectiveness and information security. The network is the combat multiplier for our globally responsive and regionally engaged Army with a goal of agile and expeditionary tactical command posts supported by robust home station architecture. Army Cyber efforts reach into Electronic Warfare (EW), A-PNT, and Information Assurance in many programs.

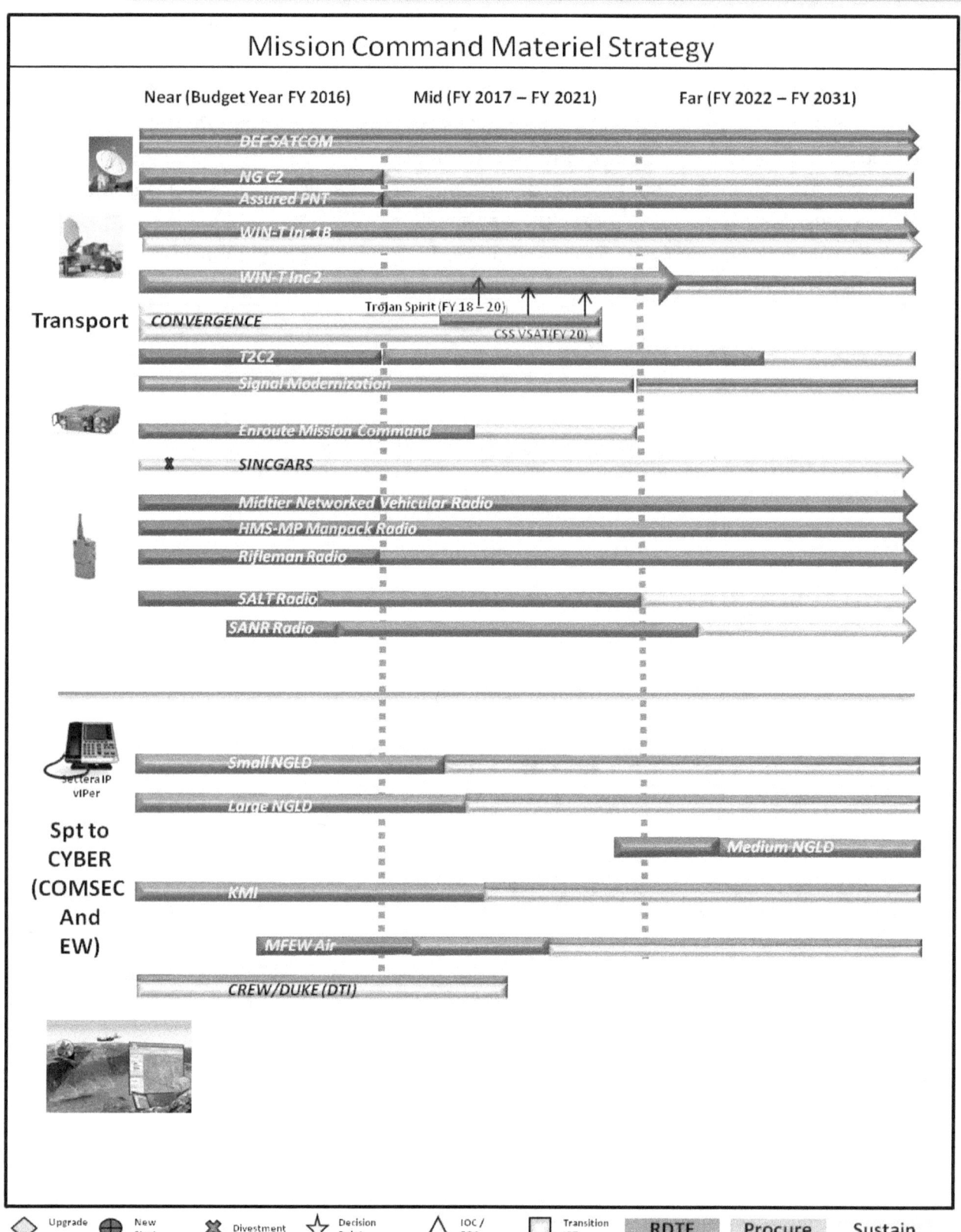

Figure 5. Mission Command (See acronym glossary)

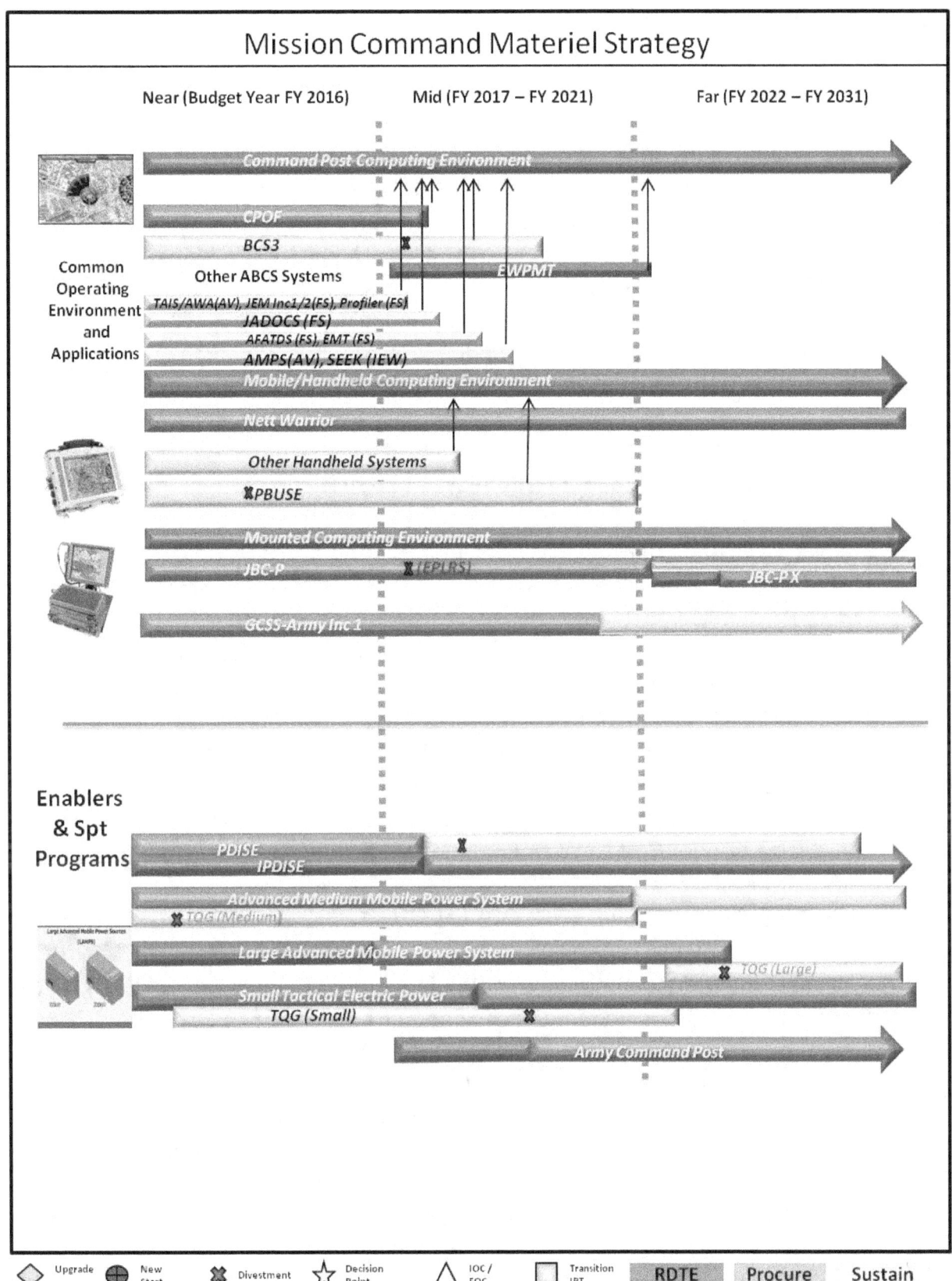

Mission Command Materiel Strategy

Near (Budget Year FY 2016) Mid (FY 2017 – FY 2021) Far (FY 2022 – FY 2031)

Common Operating Environment and Applications

- Command Post Computing Environment
- CPOF
- BCS3
- Other ABCS Systems
- EWPMT
- TAIS/AWA(AV), JEM Inc1/2(FS), Profiler (FS)
- JADOCS (FS)
- AFATDS (FS), EMT (FS)
- AMPS(AV), SEEK (IEW)
- Mobile/Handheld Computing Environment
- Nett Warrior
- Other Handheld Systems
- PBUSE
- Mounted Computing Environment
- JBC-P
- [EPLRS]
- JBC-P X
- GCSS-Army Inc 1

Enablers & Spt Programs

- PDISE
- IPDISE
- Advanced Medium Mobile Power System
- TQG (Medium)
- Large Advanced Mobile Power System
- TQG (Large)
- Small Tactical Electric Power
- TQG (Small)
- Army Command Post

Legend: ◇ Upgrade ● New Start ✖ Divestment ☆ Decision Point △ IOC / FOC ☐ Transition IPT RDTE Procure Sustain

Figure 6. Mission Command (See acronym glossary)

Section II. Strategy Update

Budget reductions have impacted the Mission Command portfolio. To support an effective and efficient network with fewer resources the Army accepted risk through programmatic restructure and delays. The Army will continue fielding critical capabilities through Capability Sets (CS) to Brigade Combat Teams at a reduced annual rate from 4 to 3 BCTs, continue NIEs to achieve Network 2020 objectives and set conditions for Network 2025 development, and accept risk by restructuring WIN-T Increment 3 to complete the high band waveform and a common NetOps tool for integration across the network while deferring an aerial layer. Efforts also include testing and procurement of a wideband mid-tier radio capability for both the ground and aerial forces and planning for development of an electronic warfare planning tool and electronic warfare offensive capability.

Section III. Portfolio Accomplishments (FY 2014 / 2015)

- Fielding of Operational Capability Set 14 (CS14) to five Brigade Combat Teams and one Division headquarters and fielding Operational Capability Set 15 (CS15) to four Brigade Combat teams and two Division Headquarters. CS14/15 provides the integrated networking on-the-move capability through networking radios, satellite systems, software applications and smart phone like devices developed as a result of Soldier-driven evaluations during the NIE process.
- As of 30 Oct 14, 63 percent of the WIN-T Increment 1 modifications have been completed. These modifications upgrade all WIN-T Increment 1 units to Increment 1b to provide enhanced networking at the halt capabilities by introducing the Net Centric Waveform modem and the colorless core for interoperability.
- High Capacity Line of Sight (HCLOS) AN/TRC-190C (V) 1 & 3 is an at-the-halt capability employed with WIN-T Increment 1 and will be retained in the Corps, Battlefield Surveillance Brigade (BfSB), Maneuver Enhancement Brigade (MEB), Sustainment Brigades and Engineer Support Battalion (ESB) formations. It's an Ultra High Frequency (UHF) Line of Sight (LOS) radio relay/transmitter-receiver fielded with the Command Post Node (CPN) and Joint Network Nodes (JNN). Current upgrade of capability includes extending the range capacity and transmission capability from 8 to16 Mbps with upgrades planned through FY 2016.
- Conducted the Follow-on Operational Test and Evaluation (FOTE) #2 for WIN-T Increment 2, providing an initial on-the-move capability and extending the network to the company level. Fielded initial Increment 2 to support CS14 Brigade Combat Teams and Division Headquarters.

- In FY 2015, under WIN-T Increment 3, demonstrated the Highband Networking Waveform (HNW) 3.0 which supports the Joint Aerial Layer Network (JALN) and begins NetOps build 4/5.
- Continued to execute fielding of Rifleman Radio (RR) and initial fielding of Handheld, Manpack and Small Form Fit (HMS) Manpack in support of CS14/15. Conduct follow on limited user test NIE 15.2.
- Changed acquisition strategy for HMS product of Manpack and RR to address full and open competitive multi-vendor contract award. RR Request for Proposal (RFP) was released for selection of competing vendors for performance evaluation and qualification testing. RR full rate production is planned for FY16. HMS Manpack RFP released in 1st Quarter (QTR) FY 2015 to support vendor down select for performance evaluation and testing. HMS Manpack Full Rate Production planned for FY 2017. Completed development of Command Post of the Future (CPOF) version 7.0 that supports continuous operations in all network environments and sets conditions for the Command Post Computing Environment (CP CE) which is part of the COE. Conducted an operational evaluation at NIE 14.1 in support of a fielding decision. Beginning with fielding in FY 2014, CPOF V 7.0 provides the ability to operate in disconnected, intermittent and latent network environments and automatically re-synchronizes offline data changes when the network becomes available.
- Completed development and testing of JBC-P systems providing significant improvements in situational awareness, mission command collaboration, patrol planning and logistics management tools. The first unit fielding is scheduled January 2015 and to the rest of the force, starting in 2016. The program has continued the convergence of all users to Blue Force Tracking and the divestiture of the Enhanced Position Location and Reporting System (EPLRS) radios.
- Continued development of the CP CE under the COE, which provides a significantly enhanced Common Operating Picture (COP) and collaboration through a common web interface on a consolidated Mission Command workstation for maneuver, intelligence, fires, aviation, air defense, and logistics management tools and applications in a more intuitive and cost effective manner. The COE V3 effort was formalized by Headquarters, Department of the Army (HQDA) G-3 COE order and by the Army Acquisition Executive System of Systems directive assigning lead responsibilities for various Computing Environments (CE), which includes the CP CE as well as the Mounted and Mobile/Hand Held CEs. CP CE V1 was taken to NIE 14.2 for assessment to support the acceleration of COE development.
- Successfully integrated National Security Agency (NSA) approved next generation pilot Crypto Key Material management test account systems across the force.

- Continued bi-annual NIE events that tested program of record systems, validated integration of the Operational Capability Sets, and demonstrated new technologies in accordance with the Army's Agile Process standardized operating procedure. During NIEs 14.1, 14.2, and 15.1 conducted multiple Systems Under Test (SUTs), Systems Under Evaluation (SUEs) and Demonstrations. Beginning with NIE 15.2, all following (x.2) events will be solely focused on required testing of programs of record supporting Network 2020 objectives.

- Continued the modernization of Army's tactical electrical power generators and the air conditioner fleet through the fielding of Advanced Medium Mobile Power Sources (AMMPS) and the associated power distribution systems as well as the Improved Environmental Control Units (IECU). Plans are to continue AMMPS fielding through FY25. This fleet-wide generator modernization is expected to result in 15-21 percent reduction of the fuel consumption over the legacy generators. Meanwhile, the AMMPS that were fielded to Afghanistan are being brought back for reset and reissue. Regarding IECUs, as of October 2014, 1660 have been fielded. These IECUs replaced Army's legacy air conditioners that use ozone depleting chemicals with Environmental Protection Agency (EPA) approved refrigerants. The IECU modernization effort is to continue through 2020 to comply with EPA mandates.

Section IV. Key FY 2016 Mission Command Investments

The FY 2016 Mission Command investments total $2.78B ($530.9M RDTE / $2.11B OPA / $133.6M OMA) and includes communications transport, applications and network services capabilities. Specific investments in this portfolio include:

- $504.5M (OPA) procures WIN-T Increment 2, providing broadband backbone communications, equipping three BCTs, three Division Headquarters, six battalions realigned to BCTs as part of force structure changes, and supports previously procured assets.

- $39.7M (RDTE) continues the development of WIN-T Increment 3 integrated NetOps, Highband Networking Waveform and NetCentric Waveform 10.x increasing network flexibility and tailorability.

- $8.8M (RDTE) supports Mid-Tier Networking Vehicular Radio (MNVR) systems testing and evaluation events to support production and fielding decisions. As part of the Family of Tactical Radios, MNVR, like Rifleman Radio, provides advanced joint tactical end-to-end networking data and voice communications.

- $34.9M (OPA) supports 300 Rifleman Radio operational test assets in FY 2016.

- $49.8M (OPA) procures and supports Nett Warrior fielding to meet dismounted leader command and control/situation awareness networking requirements for FY 2016 and FY17 Operational Capability Set BCTs.
- $133.3M (OPA) procures JBC-P, enabling Mission Command on the move, for approximately 30 BCTs and Brigade size formations, including replacement of EPLRS in BCTs.
- $12.4M (RDTE) supports implementation of Mounted Computing Environment (MCE) as part of COE to enable rapid application development and interoperability.
- $70.5M (RDTE) resources developmental efforts for Command Post Computing Environment to implement COE and provide the server infrastructure to support COE V3 fielding in FY19. This effort delivers command post capabilities interoperable with other computing environments and converges/simplifies mission command onto a cyber hardened common server infrastructure with standardized common services supported by a unified data strategy.
- $162.6M (OPA) continues user license procurement, training and fielding of GCSS-A Increment 1 Wave 2/Army Enterprise Systems Integration Program (AESIP) consisting of unit supply, ground maintenance and property book functionality.
- $12.3M (RDTE) continues remaining operational testing and system integration for GCSS-A Increment 1, AESIP Increment 1 and the beginning of the build of Business Intelligence/Business Warehouse for GCSS-A Increment 2.
- $30.1M (RDTE) starts the developmental effort for the Assured PNT program, protecting unhindered access to PNT information.
- $8.6M (RDTE) initiates development and testing of an Electronic Warfare Planning and Management Tool (EWPMT), which will assist commanders during planning, coordination, and synchronization of electronic warfare on the battlefield.
- $2.6M (OPA) procures first capability drop of EWPMT.
- $196.7M (OPA) for the continued modernization of Army's tactical electrical power generation and air conditioner fleet.
- $99.2M (RDTE) resources the size and scope of the annual NIE, designed to keep pace with rapid advances in communications technologies and deliver proven and integrated network capabilities to Soldiers.

INTELLIGENCE

Section I. Overview

The Intelligence Portfolio incorporates key components of intelligence collection, exploitation and analysis across four primary layers: Foundation, Terrestrial, Aerial and Space. The goal of the portfolio is to fully integrate the core intelligence capabilities, including Signals Intelligence (SIGINT) collection, Counterintelligence (CI), Human Intelligence (HUMINT) interrogation and source operations and Geospatial Intelligence (GEOINT), including Full Motion Video (FMV). The portfolio also includes secure intelligence communications architecture, synchronized and integrated with the Army's network initiatives. This architecture supports all aspects of processing, exploitation, analysis and dissemination of intelligence to meet the readiness and modernization objectives of The Army Plan.

Section II. Strategy update

Based on fiscal constraints and unforecasted operational requirements, the Intelligence Portfolio procurement strategy has been modified to ensure combatant commands have the intelligence they need to win in a complex world. The rate at which the Army provides enhanced Distributed Common Ground System-Army (DCGS-A) capabilities, training and hardware refresh to units has been extended from three to five years with the rate of software baseline releases remaining every 36-48 months. This will resource and maintain an advanced analytics capability that leverages Cloud computing. To keep pace with the rapidly evolving communications environment, we will maintain and modernize the terrestrial SIGINT collection capability with Prophet Enhanced. The Army's manned Aerial Intelligence, Surveillance and Reconnaissance (ISR) capabilities have been maintained and aligned with the Army's Military Intelligence (MI) 2020 strategy. Additionally, we will modernize and integrate our manned Aerial ISR platforms to include emerging sensors through upgrades and replacements and in the Far Term we will look to a next generation Aerial ISR Platform based upon the Economic Useful Life (EUL) of our existing fleet. We will provide a range of sensor payloads to support Unmanned Aircraft Systems (UAS) platforms to meet the requirements for persistent surveillance and Reconnaissance, Surveillance and Target Acquisition (RSTA). We will continue to leverage the capacity of Intelligence Community in the Space Layer with development of Tactical Exploitation of National Capabilities (TENCAP) and Theater Net-Centric Geolocation.

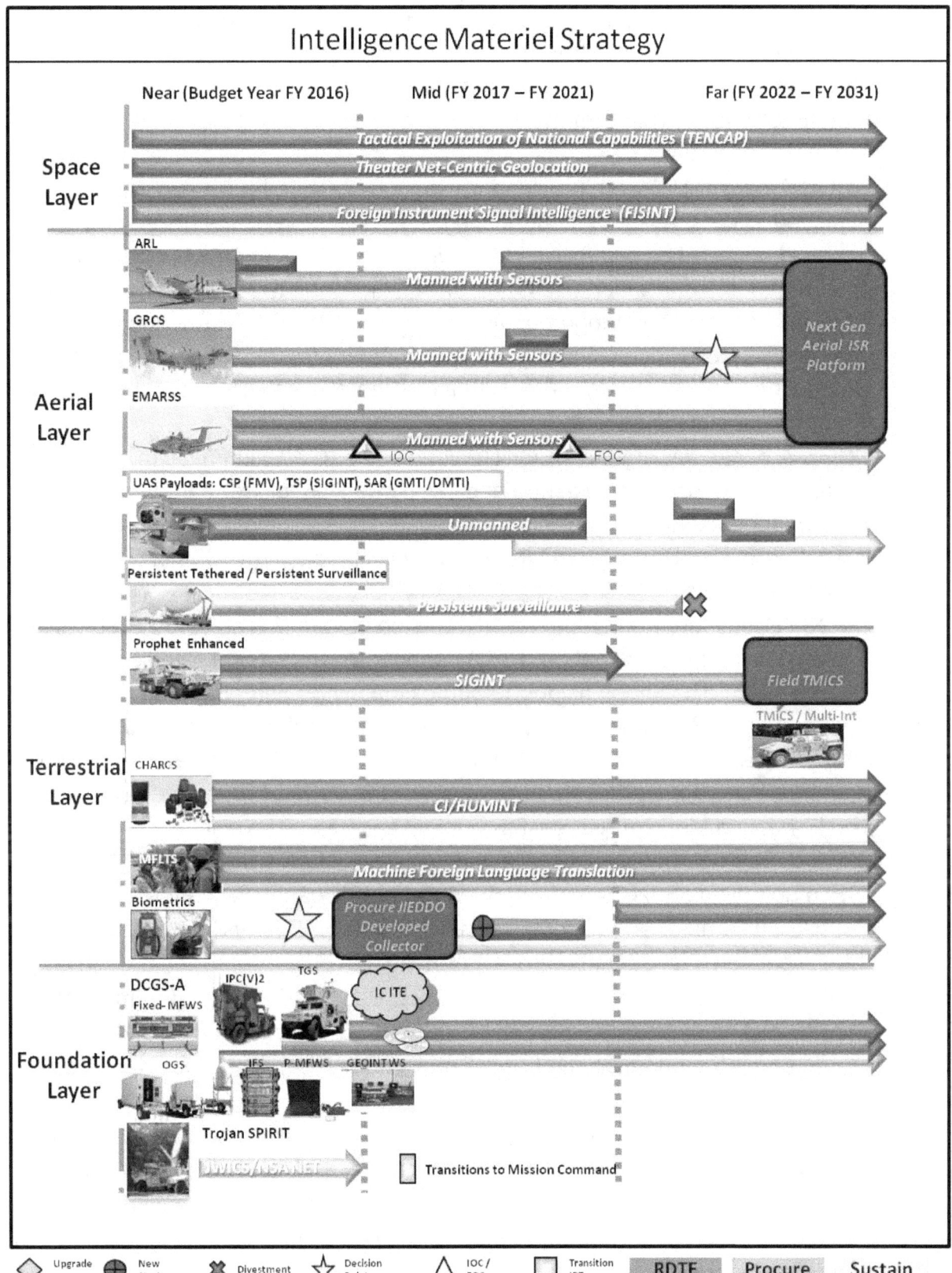

Figure 7. Intelligence (see acronym glossary)

As depicted in figure 7, the Intelligence portfolio provides essential modernization to keep pace with the evolving threat and rapid technological advancements.

Section III. Portfolio Accomplishments (FY 2014 / 2015)

- DCGS-A capabilities were provided to Headquarters 101st Air Assault Division deployed to West Africa in response to the Ebola outbreak in FY 2014. It provided unclassified capabilities to establish a U.S., host nation, and non-governmental organization (NGO) medical situational awareness and geospatial information network to support unified operations. DCGS-A continued Operations/Intelligence Convergence development for the Command Post Computing Environment (CP CE) with incremental assessments at the Network Integration Evaluation events in FY 2014.
- DCGS-A began fielding the GEOINT Workstation (GWS) in FY 2014. The GWS integrates Geospatial Intelligence and Topographic engineer capabilities in a reduced footprint and is displacing the Digital Topographical Support System (DTSS) Family of Systems and the Imagery Workstation (IWS) Quick Reaction Capability (QRC).
- DCGS-A Hunte software baseline provides enhanced ISR software Processing, Exploitation and Dissemination (PED) capabilities and incorporates ease of use aspects. Hunte has been fielded to approximately 36 percent of the Force on the Secret Internet Protocol Router (SIPR) network. It is the foundation of the software that will be tested in 3rd QTR FY 2015 and will begin fielding on Top Secret/Special Compartmented Information (TS/SCI) networks in early FY 2016.
- The Enhanced Medium Altitude Reconnaissance and Surveillance System (EMARSS) program achieved Milestone C and Capability Production Document (CPD) approved for the Army's manned Aerial ISR capability, in FY 2014.
- EMARSS Instructor and Key Personnel Training (IKPT) and Limited Users Test (LUT) scheduled for January through April 2015.
- Continued to prepare the Guardrail Common Sensor (GRCS) program for the FMV testing and integration on 14 RC-12X GRCS systems in FY 2014.
- The Airborne Reconnaissance Low - Enhanced (ARL-E) CPD was approved in FY 2014.
- ARL-E was maintained and system software, payloads and workstations were upgraded to sustain ARL ISR collection capability and relevance in FY 2014.
- Continued preparations for ARL program to transition to an Enhanced capability (ARL-E) by leveraging QRCs currently supporting Operation Freedom's Sentinel (OFS).
- Equipped the MQ-1 Gray Eagle UAS platform with Common Sensor Payload (CSP) and the Small Tactical Radar-Lightweight (STARLite) sensors in FY 2014

and FY 2015. CSP is a turreted, multi-sensor Electro-Optic/Infrared/Laser Designator (EO/IR/LD) system that provides day/night FMV imaging. STARLite is a Synthetic Aperture Radar/Ground Moving Target Indicator (SAR/GMTI) capability that provides imagery through weather and detects moving target indicators. Production commenced on High Definition (HD) CSP, an upgrade that will be fielded to the U.S. Army Special Operations Forces (SOF) and Aerial Exploitation Battalions (AEB). Development provided software to improve STARLite sensor processing and exploitation and Tactical SIGINT Payload (TSP) Block I and test activities. TSP is an Aerial SIGINT collection sensor under development for the MQ-1 Gray Eagle UAS that detects radio frequency emitters.

- Fielded the Army's ground SIGINT collection capability, Prophet Enhanced, a more modular and vehicle-agnostic version to Multi-Function Teams (MfT) within BCTs and Battlefield Surveillance Brigades (BfSB) / Enhanced MI Brigades (EMIB) operating in combat theaters in FY 2014 and FY 2015.

Section IV. Key FY 2016 Intelligence Investments

The FY 2016 Intelligence portfolio investments total $737.8M ($227.5M Aircraft Procurement, Army (ACFT) / $149.2M RDTE / $361.1M OPA) and include the key components of ISR tasking, collection, exploitation and analysis. Specific investments in this portfolio include:

- $285.9M ($25.6M RDTE / $260.3M OPA) funds DCGS-A development and procurement to modernize and procure components for the DCGS-A systems and setting conditions for the Army's ISR component of the COE. DCGS-A hardware and software will be integrated into select ISR current force platforms to network enable and provide enhanced ISR PED capabilities. DCGS-A RDTE will fund the correction of deficiencies discovered during the 3rd QTR FY 2015 LUT and integrate software baselines that can begin fielding in 2016 on both SIPR and TS/SCI networks. It also will fund preparations for the DCGS-A Increment 2 milestone decision and begin Increment 2 development and testing. Increment 2 will develop and test DCGS-A multi-intelligence capable software baselines and the CP CE as it fits into the Army's overarching COE construct. Additionally, development provides for iterative software releases that increase the PED the Army requires and continues critical updates and overarching intelligence processing capability to the Army through the cloud computing capability. The approach will achieve information technology efficiencies through the alignment with Intelligence Community Information Technology Environment. DCGS-A procurement provides 11 Tactical Intelligence Ground Stations (TGS), two Operational Intelligence Ground Stations (OGS), four Intelligence Processing

Centers (IPC) (V) 1, 16 IPC (V) 2, 134 GWS, 200 Intelligence Fusion Servers (IFS), 1,620 DCGS-A Portable Multi-Function Workstations (P-MFWS), and Commercial off the Shelf (COTS) software licenses to enhance performance of fielded systems and support the integration of Intelligence Community investments. These systems will support one Corps, three Divisions, 12 BCTs, two SOF units, four Maneuver Enhancement Brigades, four Combat Aviation Brigades (CABs), three Fires Brigades and other Combat Support (CS) and Combat Service Support (CSS) units entering the force generation available pool and institutional training units.

- $32.7M ($5.3M RDTE / $27.3M ACFT) Provides non-recurring engineering cost associated with aircraft integration and mission equipment package (MEP) enhancements, modifies the aircraft to include Engineer, Furnish and Install (EF&I) of modifications as a complete contractual effort for EMARSS. Provides Sensor Engineering Change Proposals (ECP) and contractor system support, matrix engineering support for sensor enhancements, Systems Engineering and Technical Assistance (SETA), and data testing and corrective actions resulting from Operational Tests. Provides for procurement and installation of EMARSS modifications, and other associated costs to enhance the Army's persistent capability to detect, locate, classify/identify, and track surface targets in day/night and near-all weather conditions with a high degree of timeliness and accuracy. Provides Program Management Office Support, Engineering Support, Engineering Changes, System Test and Evaluation, Depot Facilitation, and Initial Fielding Support.

- $17.5M (ACFT) provides for upgrade of eight FMV systems and installation of four onto four aircraft, fielding and training for GRCS. Additionally, supports airframe upgrades to communications, navigation, and surveillance systems to meet Global Air Traffic Management (GATM) requirements.

- $102.4M ($17.6M RDTE / $84.8M ACFT) funds Long Range Radar (LRR) development effort. Procures ten components for build of two mission equipment packages (MEP), consisting of two DCGS-A workstations, three sets of communication equipment, one communications intelligence (COMINT) subsystem, and four FMV subsystems. Additionally, supports effort to upgrade Quick Reaction Capability (QRC) DHC-8 300 aircraft with universal cockpits and aircraft survivability equipment (ASE).

- $108.2M ($10.7M RDTE / $97.5M ACFT) for UAS ISR Payloads, providing the MQ-1C Gray Eagle platform with day and night capability to collect and display FMV continuous imagery, wide-area all-weather search capability, persistent stare, GMTI and SAR capabilities. Supports Interim Contractor Support (ICS) for CSP and STARLite and provides initial fielding of 27 CSPs and 27 STARLites. Procures 18 CSPs, 18 STARLites and 15 TSP sensors, initial spares, contractor logistics support, integration and fielding support to SOF and AEBs. Provides RDTE for CSP development efforts to increase tactical utility, operational effectiveness and reduce operator workload for CSP as well as STARLite Sensor Processing and Exploitation (SPE) software development test and integration onto Gray Eagle. Provides TSP system engineering, testing and support for MQ-1C.

- $74.3M ($6.7M RDTE / $67.6M OPA) for Prophet Ground SIGINT. Development provides product upgrades for next-generation signals for pre-planned product improvement requirements for Prophet Enhanced sensors. Modernizes 14 Prophet Enhanced sensors for training and fielding to MfTs in BCTs and EMIBs. Funding will also procure 10 next generation receivers and hardware/software improvements to enhance SIGINT exploitation and keep pace with rapidly changing threat technology, tactics, techniques and procedures.

MANEUVER

Section I. Overview

The Maneuver Portfolio's goal is to develop and field an integrated combined team capable of dominating across the range of missions today and into the future. Key to this effort is our Combat Vehicle Modernization Strategy which transforms the capability of the Brigade Combat Team. The strategy as depicted in figure 8, replaces the M113 Family of Vehicles with an Armored-Multi Purpose Vehicle (AMPV) in Armored Brigade Combat Teams (ABCT), improves the Abrams tank, the Bradley Fighting Vehicles and the Stryker with increased mobility and protection.

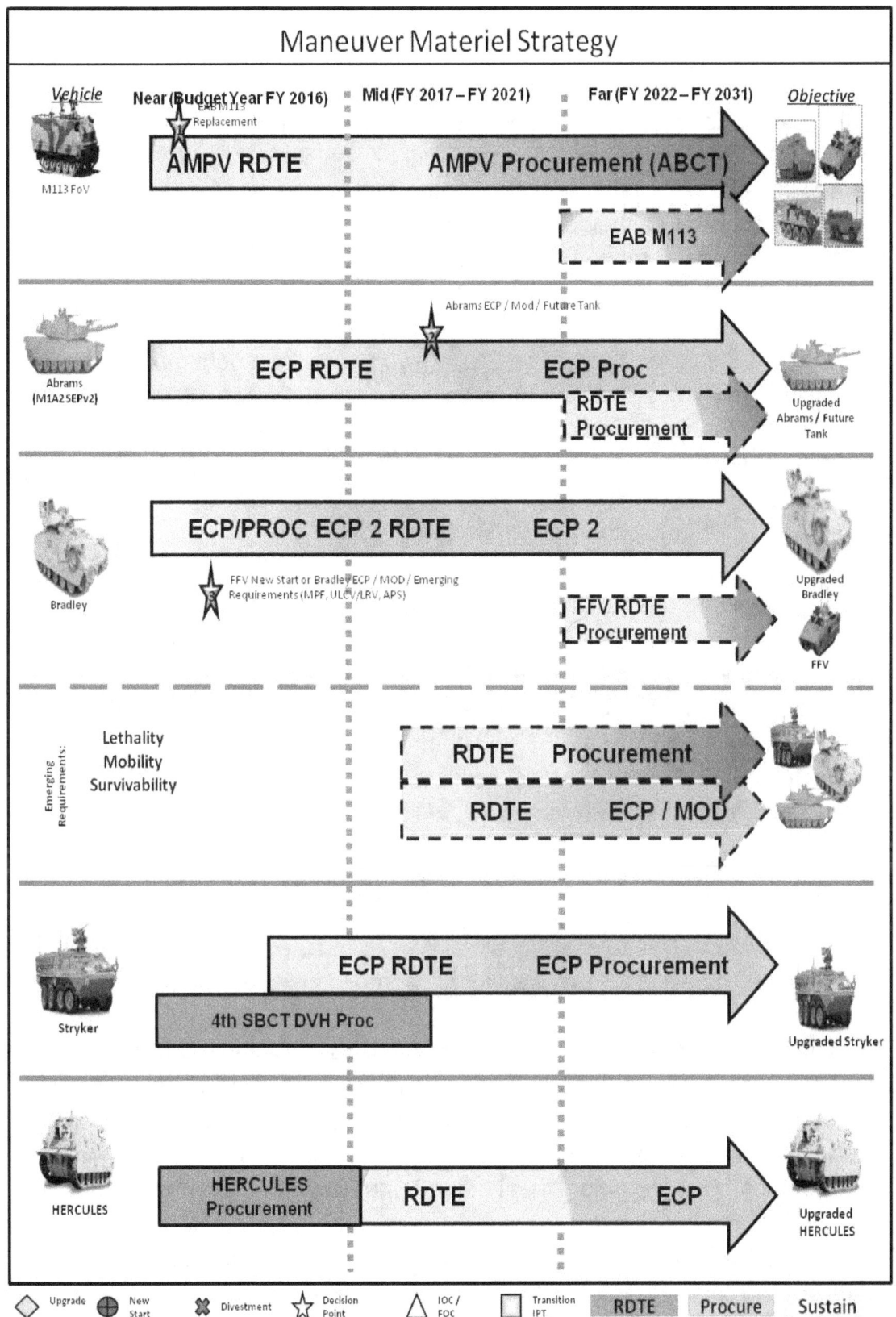

Figure 8. Maneuver (see acronym glossary)

Section II. Strategy Update

Based on current fiscal constraints and the introduction of a new Army Operating Concept, the Combat Vehicle Portfolio modified its strategy to focus funding in the near term on the Army's proven platforms (Abrams, Bradley and Stryker) and the development of the AMPV. This strategy keeps the AMPV program funded to the Cost Assessment and Program Evaluation (CAPE) Independent Cost Estimate (ICE) to insure the AMPV is fielded to the force as rapidly as possible. The M113 supporting Family of Vehicles (FOV) does not possess sufficient force protection, mobility, and electrical power to sustain current or future operations. AMPV is a key component of the Army's Combat Vehicle Modernization Strategy to provide the right mix of mobility, lethality and protection across combat formations. Proven platforms will receive much needed Engineering Change Proposals (ECP) to regain lost Size/Space, Weight, Power and Cooling (SWaP-C).

Section III. Portfolio Accomplishments (FY 2014 / 2015)

- The Army approved the procurement of a 4th brigade set of Double V-Hull (DVH) with ECP Strykers. The DVH procurement leverages the DVH exchange program that converts flat bottom hull Strykers into DVHs at a significant cost savings to the Army. The DVH significantly improves crew protection in Improvised Explosive Device (IED) environments. The AMPV program entered the Engineering and Manufacturing Development (EMD) Phase in FY 2015 after a successful Milestone B decision in December 2014.

Section IV. Key FY 2016 Maneuver Investments

The FY 2016 Maneuver investments total $1.77B ($1.27B WTCV / $487.4M RDTE / $0.6M OMA). Specific investments in this portfolio include:

- $230.2 (RDTE) funds AMPV. The Milestone B Defense Acquisition Board was completed in 1st QTR FY 2015 and AMPV entered the acquisition process at Milestone B. The EMD contract was awarded in December 2014. The AMPV program is focused on replacing the legacy M113s within the ABCT first with a future decision point for replacement of the remaining echelon above brigade M113s in the Army.
- $298.8M ($225.0M WTCV / $73.8M RDTE) continues production and fielding of Bradley ECP 1 for suspension and track upgrades. RDTE funds ECP 2 development, focused on network integration and enabling SWaP-C improvements for the Bradley A3 fleet.

- $105.8M (RDTE) funds Stryker DVH ECPs that address future network integration, mobility and SWaP-C. The Stryker ECP provides growth in electrical, mechanical and engine power.

- $561.1M (WTCV) funds completion of production of a 3rd Double-V-Hull (DVH) brigade and begins production of the 4th Brigade set through the Stryker Exchange Program. DVH provides enhanced underbelly protection against IED threat environments. The 4th DVH Brigade set will include power and mobility upgrades from the ECP program.

- $445.5M ($367.9M WTCV / $77.6M RDTE) Begins production of Abrams ECP hardware in support of ECP integration in FY 2017. The RDTE supports test of the ECP and integration of Improved Forward Looking Infrared (IFLIR) into the Abrams.

- $123.6M (WTCV) continues production of HERCULES to replace legacy M88A1s in the ABCT and above Brigade units in support of ABCTs.

AVIATION

Section I. Overview

The Aviation portfolio consists of core aviation programs, including utility and cargo, fixed wing mission profiles, reconnaissance/attack, Intelligence, Surveillance and Reconnaissance (ISR), Unmanned Aircraft Systems (UAS), and enabling systems that directly support aviation unit readiness which meet readiness and modernization objectives of the Army Campaign Plan.

Key objectives and decision points are:
- Fully fund and execute the Aviation Restructuring Initiative (ARI);
- Fully fund the Apache AH-64E (Apache Block III) program;
- Fully fund the CH-47F Multi-year Contract (MYC) II Contract; and
- Fully fund the UH-60M MYC 8.

Section II. Strategy Update

As the Army downsizes and facilitates incremental improvements in an environment of competing priorities and limited resources, it is necessary to restructure Army Aviation. The ARI is a comprehensive strategy to reorganize the Army's rotary wing force mix. It retains the capabilities in highest demand by our combatant commanders within reduced funding levels, and is the best approach to meet emergent and recurring civil and homeland defense requirements. The ARI equipping strategy retains the most modernized and capable aircraft while divesting the least capable aircraft. The savings gained from divesting legacy aircraft and reduced structure enables portfolio modernization. The plan equips reconnaissance and attack units with the AH-64E Apache and equips the training base with the UH-72A Lakota in lieu of the legacy OH-58A/C Kiowa and TH-67 Creek aircraft. All components receive the modernized Black Hawk UH/HH-60M, UH-60V and the CH-47F Chinook to fill their lift and cargo requirements. The restructure places all AH-64 Apache requirements in the Active Component. The restructure also allows the Reserve Component to retain 12 aviation brigades including all Chinooks, and places an additional 111 Black Hawks in the Army National Guard (ARNG), increasing the capability to support combat assault, Civil Defense, and Homeland Defense missions. This strategy is depicted in figure 9 below.

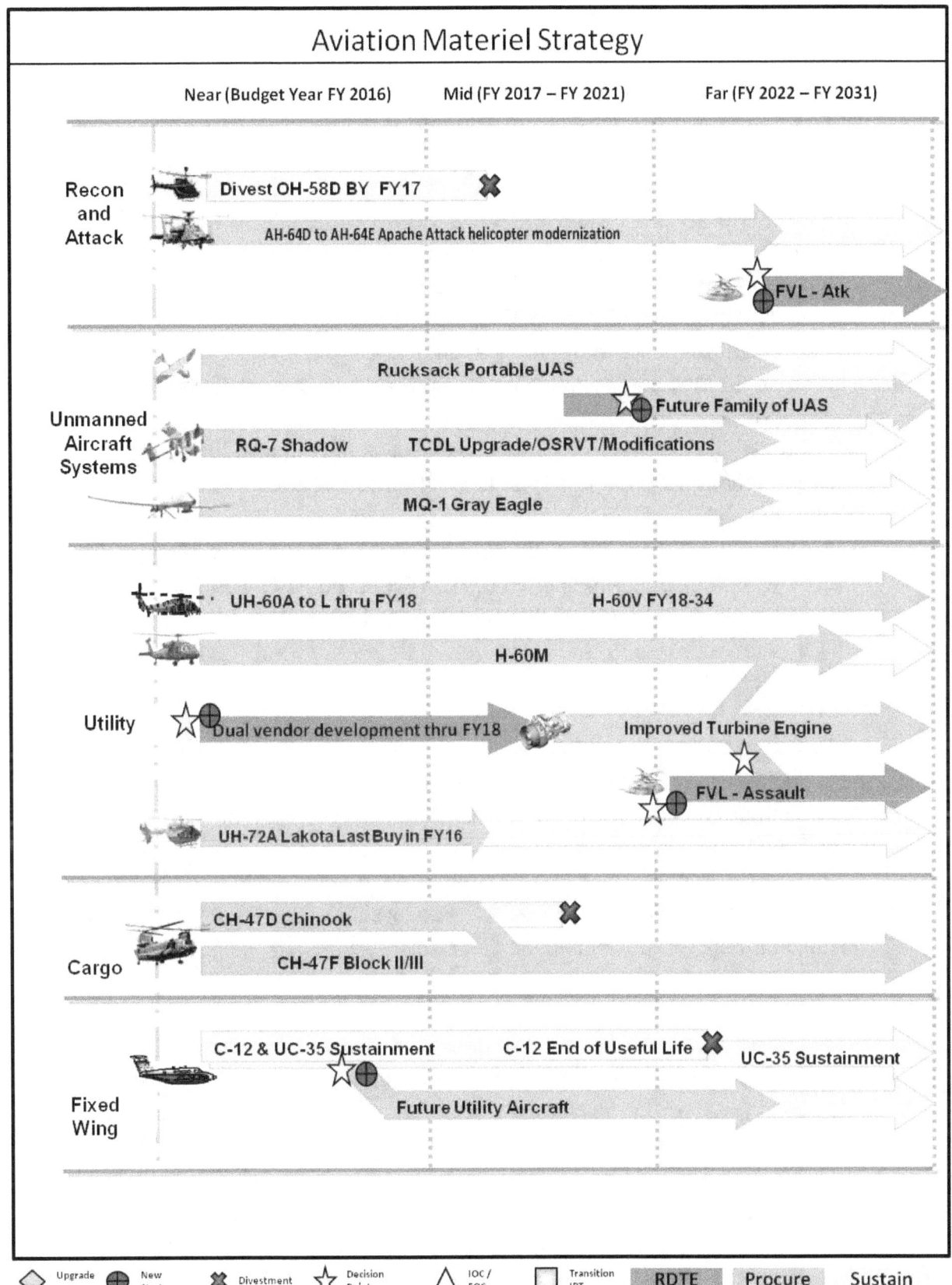

Figure 9. Aviation (See acronym glossary)

Section III. Portfolio Accomplishments (FY 2014 / 2015)

- Focused rotary wing aircraft modernization on the UH-60 (Black Hawk), CH-47 (Chinook) and AH-64 (Apache) helicopters:
- H-60:
  - ➤ Procured UH-60M (utility mission) and HH-60M (MEDEVAC mission) helicopters. The M model is a digital networked platform with greater range and lift capability to support maneuver Commanders.
  - ➤ UH-60 A/L MEDEVAC (Air) Mission Equipment Package (MEP) Project: In FY 2014, procured 42 Medical Mission Sensor Forward Looking Infrared Sensors (FLIR) and 46 Interim Patient Handling Systems. In FY 2015, will procure 20 Medical Mission Sensor FLIR and 10 Interim Patient Handling Systems.
  - ➤ Funded in FY 2014-2015 for the Black Hawk helicopter Multi Year Procurement Contract 8 (FY 2012-2016), procuring UH-60M and HH-60M aircraft.
  - ➤ FY 2014: Procured 70 H-60M aircraft (46 UH-60M, 24 HH-60M) and 37 UH-60A to UH-60L conversions; FY 2015: Procured 87 H-60M aircraft (63 UH-60M, 24 HH-60M) and 49 UH-60A to UH-60L conversions.

- CH-47F/MH-47G:

  - ➤ Procured CH-47F and MH-47G Chinook aircraft while providing modifications including a loading system enabling more rapid reconfiguration from cargo to passenger support missions. Continued fielding the CH-47F to the active and ARNG and U.S. Army Reserve components.
  - ➤ FY 2014: Procured 29 CH-47F aircraft (seven new build aircraft, 22 remanufactured aircraft); FY 2015: Procured 32 CH-47F aircraft (six new build aircraft, 26 remanufactured aircraft).

- AH-64E:

  - ➤ Procured Apache AH-64E (Apache Block III) aircraft and provided existing Block II fleet with modifications that address operationally driven improvements and obsolescence issues. Improvements: Manned-Unmanned Teaming and Sensors upgrades.
  - ➤ Continued induction of Apache AH-64D helicopters for remanufacture to AH-64E (Apache Block III); FY 2014: Procured 39 AH-64E aircraft (35 are remanufactured aircraft and four are new build aircraft); FY 2015 Procured 35 remanufactured aircraft).

- Gray Eagle Unmanned Aircraft System: FY 2014: Procured 23 MQ-1C Gray Eagle Unmanned Aircraft; FY 2015: procured 19 MQ-1C Gray Eagle Unmanned Aircraft. Gray Eagle missions include Reconnaissance, Surveillance, Target Acquisition, Armed Reconnaissance, Signals Intelligence, Communications Relay and Battle Damage Assessment.

- Shadow Unmanned Aircraft System: FY 2014: Procured Shadow modifications including eight Tactical Common Data Link (TCDL) Retrofit Kits, eight Launchers, and 25 Small Mission Computers; FY 2015: Procured Shadow modifications including 20 Tactical Common Data Link (TCDL) Retrofit Kits, 100 One System Remote Video Terminal (OSRVT) Mobile Directional Antenna Systems (MDAS), and 65 MDAS Bi-Directional Retrofit kits. New Equipment Training for TCDL Retrofits continues through FY 2020.

- Light Utility Helicopter: Procured 37 Light Utility Helicopter aircraft (UH-72A) in FY 2014 and 55 in FY 2015.

- Improved Turbine Engine Program: FY 2015: Funded $49.3M in RDT&E to support the continued development of the Improved Turbine Engine Program (ITEP).

- Fixed Wing: FY 2014: Procured two T-6 aircraft for the Army Test and Evaluation Command to replace retiring T-34 aircraft; funded fixed wing aircraft modifications for both the Operational Support Airlift and Intelligence Surveillance and Reconnaissance fleet with Global Air Traffic Management (GATM) upgrades, cockpit upgrades and mandatory safety upgrades.

- Completed Air Warrior System fielding in FY 2014.

- Fielded the Hostile Fire Quick Reaction Capability (QRC) / Generation 3 Electronics Control Unit (GEN III ECU).

- Continued equipping of the Advanced Threat Infrared Countermeasures (ATIRCM) on the CH-47F helicopters.

Section IV. Key FY 2016 Aviation Investments

FY 2016 Aviation investments total $6.0B ($5.46B ACFT / $461.2M RDTE / $11.0M OMA / $33.7M Procurement of Ammunition, Army (AMMO) / $28.0M MSLS) and includes required capabilities in the reconnaissance, attack, unmanned aerial systems, utility and cargo, fixed wing and aviation enabler systems mission profiles. Specific investments in this portfolio include:

- $77.6M (RDTE) for the Technology Development phase of the Common Infrared Countermeasure (CIRCM) system for Army aviation platforms. CIRCM is a lightweight, low cost, highly reliable laser-based countermeasure system which works in conjunction with Service missile warning systems (i.e. Common Missile Warning System (CMWS)).
- $260.4M for MQ-1C Gray Eagle procures 15 aircraft and associated ground support equipment for an additional Intelligence and Security Command company in support of the Global Force Management Allocation Plan (GFMAP).
- $88.7M ($81.4M ACFT / $7.3M RDTE) for RQ-7B Shadow supporting acquisition of four Shadow TCDL Retrofit kits (and associated spare parts), four launchers, ten OSRVT Systems, and 100 OSRVT Mobile Directional Antenna Systems.
- $1.74B ($1.62B ACFT / $117.8M[7] RDTE) procures 94 H-60M aircraft (70 UH-60M, 24 HH-60M), resources UH-60V RDTE efforts, purchases mission equipment packages, and resources 40 UH-60A to UH-60L conversions.
- $1.56B ($1.49B ACFT / $69.9M RDTE) procures 64 remanufactured AH-64E (Apache Block III) aircraft and associated modifications to existing AH-64D/E fleet.
- $1.25B ($1.21B ACFT / $37.4M RDTE) procures 39 CH-47F aircraft (27 remanufactured aircraft, 12 New Build CH-47F aircraft) and associated modifications to the Chinook fleet.
- $187.2M (ACFT) procures 28 new build UH-72A Lakota Light Utility Helicopters (LUH) to assume the initial entry rotary wing training helicopter requirement and to assist in the transition to the restructured aviation force.

---

[7] Includes $51.2M RDTE for Improved Turbine Engine Program

INDIRECT FIRES

Section I. Overview

To win in a complex world future Army Indirect Fires provide adaptable indirect fires. This provides a versatile mix of Indirect Fires capabilities at the strategic, operational and tactical echelons that are flexible, integrated, precise, responsive and effective. Indirect fires are dynamically tailored to support Army, joint, interorganizational and multinational elements while operating dispersed geographically. Indirect Fires provide agile, task organized, trained, sustainable and deployable set of capabilities to achieve timely, effective and efficient effects through the full range of operational and environmental conditions. Army Indirect Fires contributions to setting the theater include: expanded operational and strategic fires; extended range, lethality, and scalability of Indirect Fires systems; joint interorganizational and multinational Indirect Fires integration; targeting; and combat identification and target location to establish and maintain the conditions necessary to retain joint force freedom of action. The Indirect Fires integrated portfolio consists of weapons platforms, mission command software, fire support sensors, and target locating devices and precisions munitions that identify targets to deliver operationally adaptable Indirect Fires in support of combined arms operations. (See figure 10).

To meet the threats of an ever adaptive adversary who employs unconventional tactics, the Army must carefully balance the quantity, quality and management of its equipment.

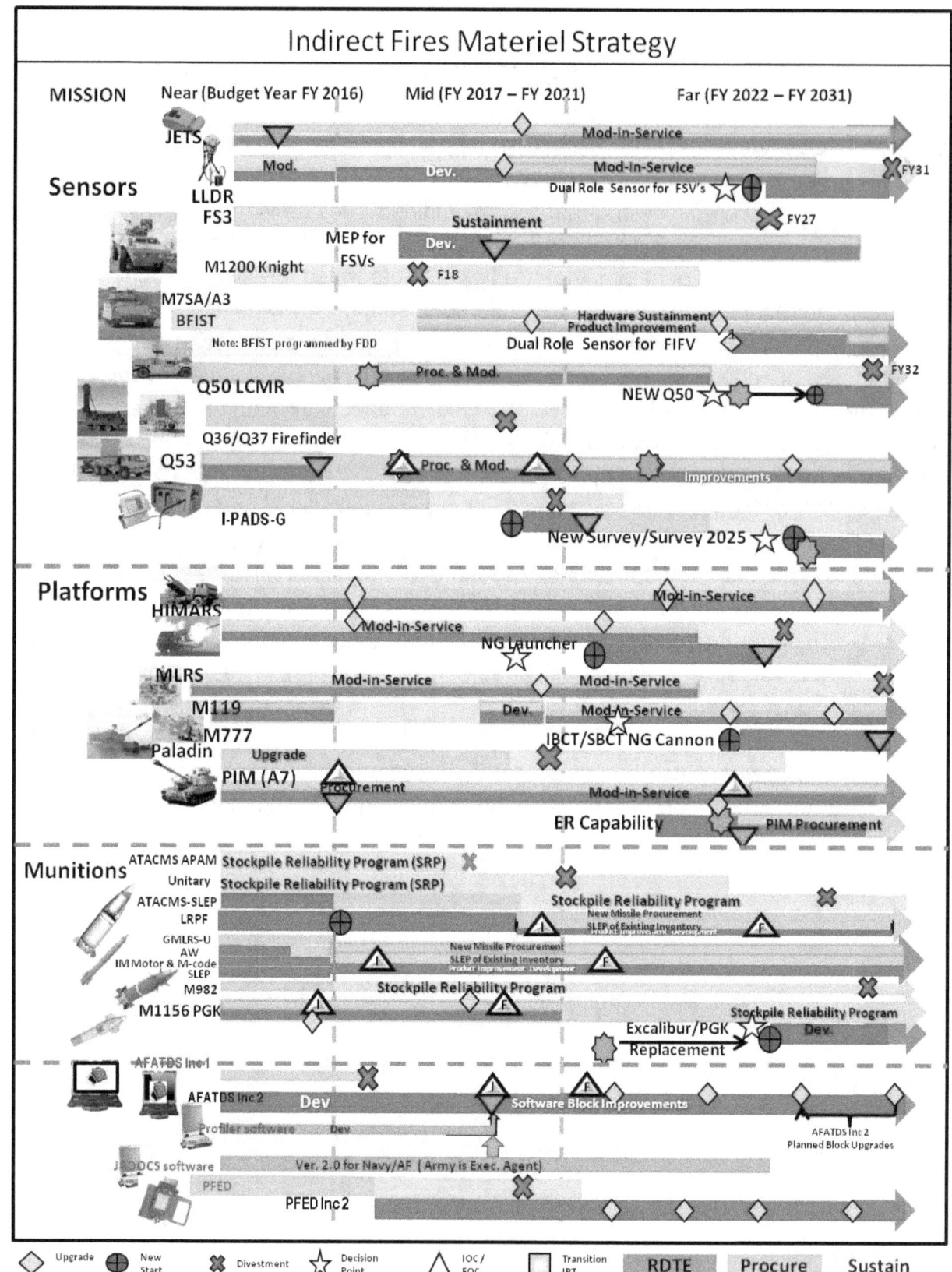

Figure 10. Indirect Fires (see acronym glossary)

The Indirect Fires portfolio includes several types and variants of equipment, which focuses on a vast number of precision and near-precision indirect Fire missions. To that end, the key strategic objectives for the Indirect Fires portfolio continue to be:

- Improve Precision Targeting capability, especially lightweight, handheld targeting systems.
- Incorporate Joint Fires into procurement planning.
- Develop and procure Precision and Near-Precision Munitions supporting Total Army Munitions Requirements.
- Enhance organic Precision and Near-Precision Fires capabilities of Infantry Brigade Combat Teams (IBCT).
- Sustain and modernize firing platforms in synchronization with Army modernization plans.
- Support command and control program merge into the Battle Command Network architecture.
- Seek Common User Interface across all Fires launch and radar systems.
- Seek fielding opportunities in providing technologies rapidly to the Soldier.

Section II. Strategy Update

Modernization efforts will be guided by four objective Indirect Fires force characteristics: commonality, expeditionary, agile and network enabled all included in a leaner and optimized Army Indirect Fires force structure.

- Budget constraints have caused adjustments within the Precision Fires portfolio, mainly a reduction in the number of Guided Multiple-Launch Rocket System (GMLRS) rockets procured.
- Modernization and modification efforts for towed howitzers and fire support sensors will be slightly increased and we will begin a service life extension program for Army Tactical Missile System (ATACMS) to bridge the gap until the Army's Long-Range Precision Fires (LRPF) solution can be developed and procured.

Section III. Portfolio Accomplishments (FY 2014 / 2015)

- Began fielding Lightweight Laser Designator Rangefinder (LLDR) version 2H retrofit which adds celestial compass capability for improved target location in 2Q FY 2014.
- Continued development of the Joint Effects Targeting System (JETS) Target Location Designation with a JETS Production Decision in FY 2015.

- Procured 82 AN/TPQ-50 Lightweight Counter Mortar Radar (LCMR) systems (FY 2014).

- Completed "Big 3" modernization effort for High Mobility Artillery Rocket System (HIMARS) launchers effectively integrating Driver's Vision Enhancement (DVE), Blue Force Tracker (BFT) and Long Range Communications (LRC) (FY 2014).

- Began integration of the Multiple Launch Rocket System (MLRS) Improved Armored Cab (IAC) and the Fires Control System – Upgrade (FCS-U) (FY 2015) enabling the platform to fire the entire family of emerging precision missiles while significantly improving crew protection.

- Completed Developmental Test/Operational Test (DT/OT) for GMLRS Alternative Warhead (AW) setting the stage for a successful combined Milestone C and Full Rate Production decision (FY 2015).

- Paladin Integrated Management (PIM) program awarded Milestone C and LRIP contract in October 2013. Commenced Logistics Demonstration (LOG DEMO). Took delivery of first PIM LRIP model in March 2015. Continued fielding of M777A2 Howitzers to IBCTs which will enhance their organic precision fires capability.

- Continued fielding the digitized fire control modifications for the M119A2, 105mm Towed Howitzer addressing responsiveness of fires to support IBCTs.

- Developed, tested and began procurement of Increment 1B of the Excalibur 155mm Precision-Guided Artillery Munition.

- Completed improvement of M3A3 Bradley Fire Support Team (BFIST) Hardware/Software modifications with the Fire Support Sensor System (FS3).

- Continued modification to the M109A6 Paladin with Paladin Fire Control System (PFCS) to support ABCTs and transition to Paladin Integrated Management (PIM) program.

Section IV. Key FY 16 Indirect Fires Investments

FY 2016 Indirect Fires investments total $1.44B ($364.6M WTCV / $263.2M RDTE / $359.0M OPA / $100.8M AMMO / $357.0M MSLS) and include lethal and non-lethal fires and effects such as radars, cannons, launchers, munitions and automated enablers. Specific investments in this portfolio include:

- $4.7M (RDTE) / $22.3M (OPA) develops and procures LLDR 2H modifications enhancing target location accuracy.

- $11.0M (RDTE) provides RDTE for JETS. $47.2M (OPA) develops and procures JETS enhancing dismounted fire observers' targeting location capability.

- $63.5M (OPA) procures 36 AN/TPQ-50 LCMR systems.

- $37.0M (MSLS) continues procurement of the MLRS IAC cab and completes installation of the HIMARS Enhanced Command and Control (EC2) modification.
- $269.3M (MSLS) begins full rate production of Guided Multiple Launch Rocket System (GMLRS) Alternative Warhead (AW) as the cluster munitions policy compliant replacement to GMLRS Dual-purpose Improved Conventional Munition (DPICM); also begins modification of expiring GMLRS Unitary missiles into the more desired GMLRS AW variant.
- $66.1M ($36.0 RDTE/ $30.1 MSLS) Begins service life extension and modification of 140 expired ATACMS into a cluster munitions policy compliant unitary warhead which incorporates a height of burst fuze to better address long range area targets.
- $17.0M (RDTE) continues the developmental effort for a lower cost cluster munitions compliant long range precision replacement to the ATACMS missile.
- $20.6M (WTCV) procures and redesigned recoil systems, Power Systems Modifications, Training Devices, and durability modifications for the M119A3 Howitzer.
- $9.5M (RDTE) / $55.3M (AMMO) develops and procures Precision Guidance Kit (PGK) fuzes for 155mm non-precision munitions providing a near precision capability.
- $60.1M (WTCV) procures Paladin Fire Control System (PFCS) modification kits for M109A6 Paladin. PFCS combines the Paladin Digital Fire Control System-Replacement (PDFCS-R) and Dynamic Reference Unit Hybrid-Replacement (DRUH-R) into one modification kit. PFCS reflects a cost reduction and streamlining effort to field the PDFCS-R and DRUH-R as a single modification to the vehicle.
- $220.6M ($3.2M RDTE / $217.4M OPA) continues procurement of the AN/TPQ-53 radar system.
- $10.0M (WTCV) / $1.9M (RDTE) supports procurement and integration of hardware and training products, modernization of Digital Fire Control System components, and continued field retrofits of contracted Engineering Change Proposals (ECP) for the M777A2 howitzer.
- $426.2M ($273.9M WTCV / $152.3M RDTE) WTCV funds PIM LRIP vehicle sets. RDTE provides funding for Production Qualification Test (PQT), Initial Operational Test and Evaluation (IOT&E) and full up live fire test.

AIR AND MISSILE DEFENSE

Section I. Overview

The Air and Missile Defense (AMD) modernization strategy provides for a relevant and ready AMD capability, crucial to supporting our National Security Strategy, from defense of the Brigade Combat Team (BCT) to defense of the Homeland. Army AMD enables Army forces via joint combined arms, air-ground operations to seize and retain the initiative, prevent, and deter conflict, defeat adaptive threats and succeed in a wide range of contingencies. Army AMD contributes to providing Army foundational capabilities required by the Joint Force. The Army and joint force's increasing reliance on AMD requires active participation from across the Army and Department of Defense (DoD) in defining and developing AMD capabilities so that necessary force structure, services and AMD components are developed, acquired and integrated into the future force. AMD skill sets and technologies take years to develop. These modernization efforts will be guided by characteristics of commonality, expeditionary, agile, and network enabled all within a leaner and optimized Integrated Army AMD force structure. These objectives set the conditions for Army AMD's contributions to the joint, combined arms fight by providing persistent, integrated, all weather, ubiquitous AMD. These joint interoperable and interdependent capabilities must be flexible, adaptable, integrated and deployed to support theater and regional level missions and contingencies, while maintaining a robust and adaptable Homeland Defense.

The AMD portfolio consists of required capabilities in the following areas: mission command capabilities and capabilities to defend against ballistic missiles; manned and unmanned aircraft; and rocket, artillery and mortar, and cruise missiles.

As depicted in figure 11, key imperatives in the AMD portfolio include the Integrated Battle Command System (IBCS) development, recapitalization, obsolescence mitigation, sustainment of current systems, modernization and modification improvements, as well as fielding of new capabilities.

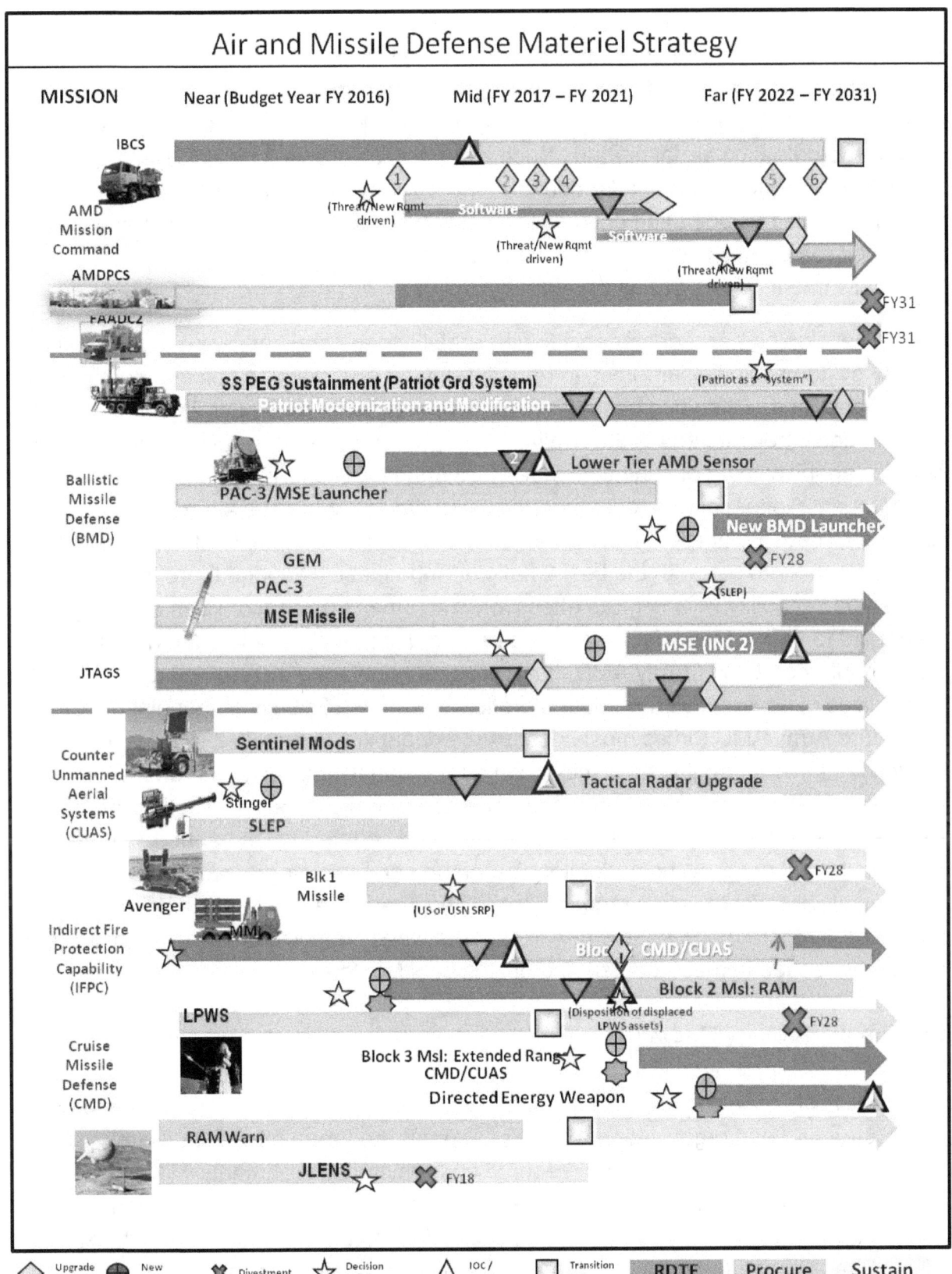

Air and Missile Defense Materiel Strategy

Figure 11. Air and Missile Defense (see acronym glossary)

Our AMD forces require a different operational approach to defending deployed forces, critical assets and our Nation against the full range of aerial threats. We can no longer afford, from a budget perspective or force structure standpoint, to match specific weapon systems against specific threats. We must take a more holistic approach when it comes to defeating aerial threats. Such an approach requires us to fully integrate through a networked, open and modular architecture whatever AMD capabilities are deployed, including Joint and potentially Coalition allies. This allows Commanders to tailor their forces to achieve the most effective and efficient mix for mission accomplishment.

Developing new components to fill capability gaps and improving, sustaining current systems allows our forces to remain relevant and ready to achieve dominance in core capabilities. Offsetting obsolescence, recapitalization and extending useful life of existing equipment increases the availability of proven systems. Moving from a system centric capability to a net centric capability will enable beyond-line-of-sight engagements, offer commanders more decision time to select the appropriate response, prevent fratricide, overcome defense design single points of failure, and allow any joint sensor to pair with the best kinetic or non-kinetic weapon. More importantly, a net centric capability will integrate effectively with other Army capabilities to allow the command to understand, visualize, describe and direct while leading and assessing throughout operations. Army AMD must focus on countering increased future capabilities of adversaries from both a proficiency and sufficiency standpoint. Present and future Army AMD forces must possess the capability to enable the defeat of a large portfolio of threats, ranging from micro unmanned aerial vehicles and mortars to cruise missiles to sophisticated short and medium range ballistic missiles. The importance of Counter-Rocket, Artillery and Mortars (C-RAM) and countering Unmanned Aircraft Systems reflect our growing understanding of the complex integrated attack which includes electronic protection requirements. The challenge, however, is how to modernize, integrate and transform AMD assets while providing the greatest depth and versatility needed to meet the demand placed on AMD forces.

Section II. Strategy Update

- As AMD capability evolves and transforms, we must ensure appropriate force structure and organizational designs support the future force with flexible and agile organizations. Future resource constrained environments will inform both capability and force structure transformation; continue to improve America's capabilities for Homeland Defense against a limited Ballistic Missile attack; and phase in needed missile defense capabilities that are responsive to the threat.
- The AMD force is currently planning and executing the most significant modernization effort in AMD history. This modernization effort will address

sensors, shooters, and mission command in an effort to quickly evolve to the threat from both state and non-state proliferators, but will also improve operational readiness due to obsolescence, while also increasing overall capacity.

- Army will field Missile Segment Enhancement (MSE) missiles to counter more sophisticate and complex threats; continue the fielding, with the Missile Defense Agency, of Terminal High Altitude Area Defense (THAAD) to improve capabilities against Medium Range Ballistic Missiles (MRBM); and continue to develop and field an integrated fire control network that can be mission tailored for quick deployment.
- Army will develop and field an Indirect Fire Protection Capability to counter UAS and cruise missile which has the ability to engage using different interceptors.

Section III. Portfolio Accomplishments (FY 2014 / 2015)

- Entered Low Rate Initial Production (LRIP) for the Patriot Advanced Capability (PAC-3) Missile Segment Enhancement (MSE) and associated launcher upgrade kits.
- Continued reset of Patriot equipment operating in the U.S. Central Command area of responsibility.
- Will complete the Lower Tier AMD Capability (LTAMDC) Analysis of Alternatives (AoA) Study that will identify next generation alternatives to modernizing the current Patriot Radar System, as well as Launchers.
- Continued providing Rocket Artillery & Mortar (RAM) sense and warn capabilities in support of Operation Enduring Freedom at 16 sites in Afghanistan.
- Continue fielding RAM warn suites to BCTs.
- Complete the transition of two active component Avenger battalions to IFPC/Avenger battalions.
- Fielded C-RAM intercept systems (Land-based Phalanx Weapon System) to two sites in Afghanistan in support of OFS. Implemented phased improvements in engagement capability per validated operational needs statement.
- Reset of 45 Air Defense and Airspace Management (ADAM) Cells and two Forward Area Air Defense Command and Control (FAAD C2) shelters.
- Fielding Air & Missile Defense Planning and Control Systems to two THAAD Batteries and one Army National Guard (ARNG) Air Defense Brigade headquarters. Additionally, fielding ADAM cells to seven Division Artillery (DIVARTY) headquarters, two Corps field artillery brigades, one ARNG Fires Brigade, one Theater Aviation Brigade, one Theater Aviation Command and five ARNG Maneuver Enhanced Brigade headquarters.

- Commence Sensor Command and Control (C2) and Enhanced Sentinel Radar fielding in accordance with Division Headquarters to Field Artillery Brigades and Division Artillery.
- Completed modernization of basic Sentinel radars to improved Sentinel radars
- Completed development of the Joint Tactical Ground Station (JTAGS) Block 2 Phase 1 prototype.
- Established the THAAD Institutional Training Base at Ft Sill.
- Completed training of THAAD Battery number three.
- Continued support of Joint Land Attack Cruise Missile Defense Elevated Netted Senor (JLENS) single orbit deployment for an exercise in FY 2015.

Section IV. Key FY 2016 Air and Missile Defense Investments

The Fiscal Year 2016 Air and Missile Defense investments total $1.64B ($660.6M RDTE / $166.4M OPA / $813.0M MSLS / $0.3M OMA) and include developing and acquiring new equipment and improving or recapitalizing current systems that offer increased capabilities; improving and increasing Patriot MSE missile inventory; conducting modification and modernization efforts of the Patriot system; conducting Service Life Extension Program (SLEP) and capability improvements on Stinger missiles; closing capability gaps, extending useful life of existing equipment; and, fielding additional THAAD batteries to provide a robust and capable Medium Range Ballistic Missile intercept capability. Specific investments in this portfolio include:

- $8.8M (RDTE) and $18.2M (OPA) supports software development and integration activities necessary to ensure compliance with Army Common Operating Environment (COE) requirements. Additionally funds necessary support activities required to complete delayed fielding of Land-based Phalanx Weapon System (LPWS) to two IFPC Avenger battalions.
- $155.4M (RDTE) $60.7M (OPA) implements the multi-block acquisition approach to provide a 360 degree, mobile, robust protection capability shifting initially from C-RAM to C-UAS and CMD. Of the total funding, $60.7M OPA provides support for fielded C-RAM systems, while RDTE is directed toward the IFPC investment.
- $55.9M ($12.3M RDTE / $43.3M OPA) continues development of software obsolescence avoidance and small/low/slow enhancements for UAS; completes application and fielding of small/low/slow for UAS and 31 Mode 5 modification upgrades to the Sentinel radars.
- $380.4M ($105.8M RDTE / $274.6M MSLS) supports U.S. commitments to the Patriot International Engineering Services program, PAC-3 field surveillance and supports and procures MSE missiles and MSE launch station upgrades. It also supports modeling, simulation, integration and tests required to assess current

and emerging threats and continue Patriot software upgrades and missile system integration.

- $596.5M ($66.4M RDTE / $530.0M MSLS) procures additional Patriot Enhanced Launcher Electronics System (ELES) launcher upgrades, continues upgrading Patriot, procures critical software upgrades to address advanced Theater Ballistic Missile (TBM) attacks, improve electronic protection capabilities, field communications upgrades and continues development of electronic warfare technology. Supports analysis of alternatives and concept development for future LTAMD sensor capability.

- $214.1M (RDTE) and $20.9M (OPA) continues Army Integrated Air and Missile Defense (AIAMD) development and enables early procurement to support initial delivery of capabilities in support of the FY 2018 IOC.

- $2.2M (MSLS) continues Proximity/Service Life Enhancement Program (PROX/SLEP) procurement; $3.1M RDTE provides for the Avenger Product Improvement Program (PIP) to address modernization and added capability.

- $24.4M ($20.5M RDTE / $3.9M OPA) supports continued development and fielding of Joint Tactical Ground Stations (JTAG) Block 2 upgrades for compatibility with new on-orbit sensors.

PROTECTION (ASSURED MOBILITY)

Section I. Overview

The Assured Mobility modernization plan procures equipment based on a validated requirement ensuring affordability and effectiveness. The portfolio focuses on an integrated suite of protection options that commanders can tailor to protect, operationally maximize and conserve unit fighting potential in Combined Arms Maneuver and Wide Area Security Operations. This supports the Army's strategic priority to support the Joint Force with critical enablers, while enroute to and operating within, expeditionary environments alongside Unified Action Partners. Additionally, it supports the combatant commanders' ability to defend the nation and its interests at home and abroad, today and against emerging threats. This portfolio emphasizes the Army's unique contributions across the range of military operations by developing systems in support of the Army Operating Concept (AOC). The Assured Mobility portfolio captures enhanced engineering abilities consistent with the functional application of these materiel solutions supporting enhanced survivability across the battlefield. Figure 12 displays a selected collection of capabilities as projected from current, near and extended term perspectives.

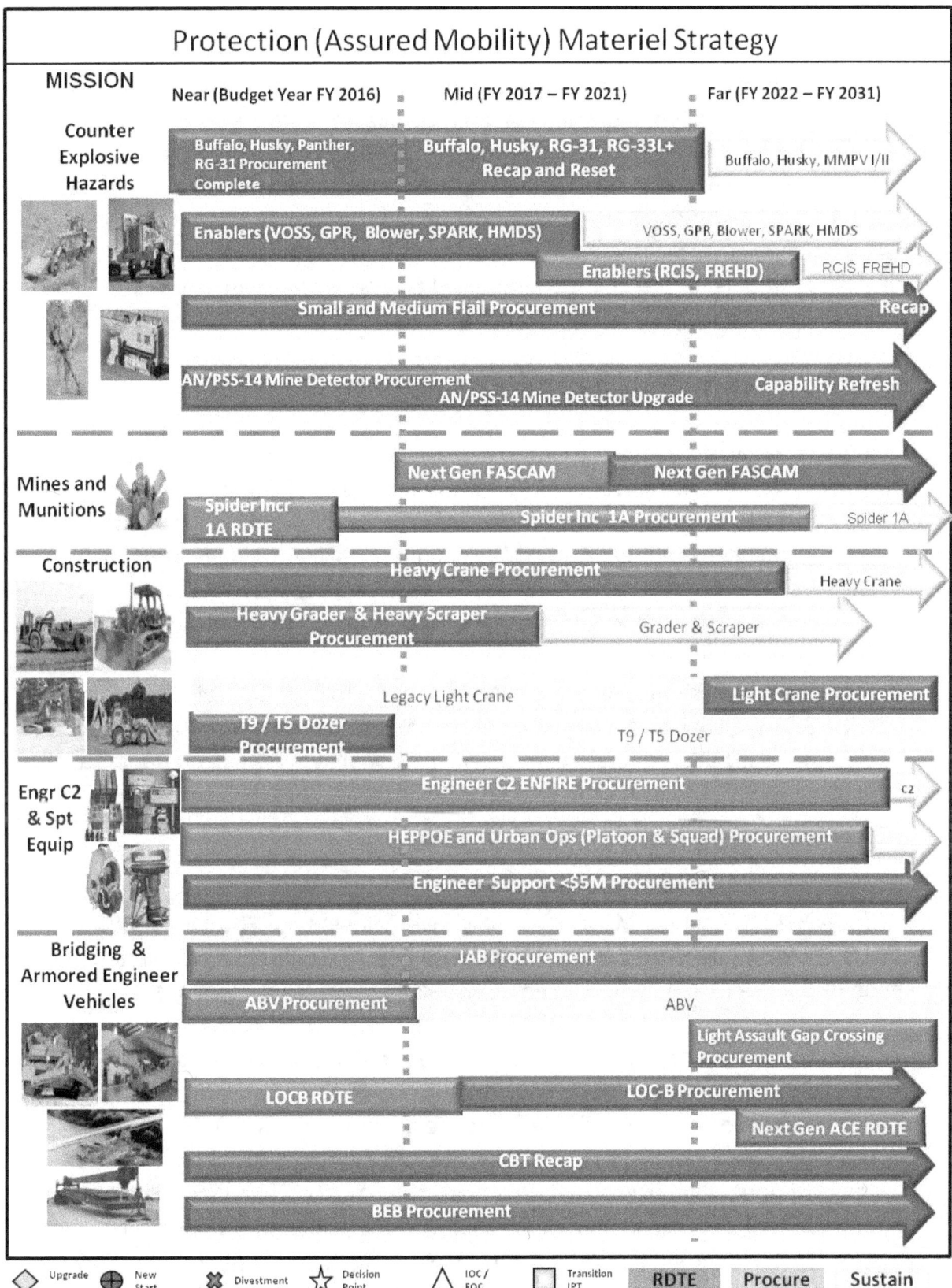

Figure 12. Protection (Assured Mobility) (see acronym glossary)

Section II. Strategy Update

Based on fiscal constraints, the portfolio strategy maintains focus on Counter Explosive Hazards (CEH) and mobility capabilities (Assault Breacher Vehicle (ABV) and Joint Assault Bridge (JAB)) that support the force. Risk was accepted by slowing procurement of Commercial-Off-The-Shelf (COTS) equipment, which includes construction equipment, and sets, kits and outfits. In addition, a recent Office of Secretary of Defense (OSD) directed Resource Management Decision (RMD) will facilitate RDTE efforts for the next generation, U.S. Policy compliant, replacement to the existing Family of Scatterable Mines (FASCAM).

Section III. Portfolio Accomplishments (FY 2014/2015)

- Fielded 98 Mine Protected Clearance Vehicles (MPCV) Buffaloes and 196 Vehicle Mounted Mine Detection (VMMD) in support of Route Clearance units.
- Fielded 17 Hydraulic Excavators, 245 Medium Dozers and 42 Heavy Scrapers; fielding continues through FY 2014. Procured 17 ABV for fielding to three ABCTs.
- Provided 527 Urban Operations Sets to platoons and squads enabling assured mobility in the urban environment.
- Provided 114 Hydraulic, Electric, Pneumatic, Petroleum Operated Equipment (HEPPOE) to support missions by clearing buildings for repair and construction, clearing areas around road construction, port openings and any other areas that require operations in an urban area.

Section IV. Key FY 2016 Assured Mobility Investments

The FY 2016 Assured Mobility portfolio investments total $662.3M ($38.9M WTCV / $117.2M RDTE / $506.2M OPA) that will ensure Soldiers are protected from multitude of battlefield and homeland security hazards. Specific investments in this portfolio include:
- $186.0M (OPA) procures 40 Medium Mine Protected Vehicles (MMPV) Type I, 86 MMPV Type II, 37 Roller/Wire Neutralization Systems (WNS) and 35 WNS into program of record configuration for fielding; upgrades 1,025 AN/PSS-14 Handheld Mine Detectors to the new Revision 6; provides $63.4M in RDTE for the next generation of standoff detection, neutralization and clearance systems.
- $33.5M (WTCV) begins procurement of four JAB's to support operational testing.
- $81.1M (OPA) procures Bridge Erection Boats (BEB) and modernizes Common Bridge Transporters (CBT) for a Multirole Bridge Company (MRBC).
- $76.9M (OPA) modernizes Heavy Scrapers, Heavy Graders, Medium Dozers

and Heavy Cranes.

- $34.5M (OPA) procures Hydraulic, Electric, Pneumatic, Petroleum Operated Equipment Hydraulic, Electric, Pneumatic, Petroleum Operated Equipment sets and 182 Urban Operations Sets.
- $16.3M (OPA) procures Instrument Set, Reconnaissance and Surveying systems to Engineer formations across the Army.
- $9.2M (OPA) procures improved Spider munition control unit.
- $50M (RDTE) initiates research and development efforts for next generation (networked / man-in-the-loop) munitions replacement for FASCAM.

PROTECTION (FORCE PROTECTION AND CHEMICAL, BIOLOGICAL, RADIOLOGICAL, NUCLEAR AND HIGH YIELD EXPLOSIVE (CBRNE)

Section I. Overview

The Force Protection portfolio focuses on an integrated suite of protection options that commanders can tailor to operationally maximize and conserve their unit fighting potential. The Force Protection Portfolio takes into consideration the extensive coordination with all portfolio stakeholders and reflects the expected priorities of future conflicts in accordance with the Army's strategic priorities to rapidly deploy, fight, sustain and win against complex state and non-state threats in austere environments and on rugged terrain employing expeditionary capabilities set forth in the Army Operating Concept (AOC). The Army prioritizes Science and Technology investments to maximize the potential of emerging game-changing land power technologies to counter emerging threats and to ensure that Army formations retain a decisive materiel edge and tactical overmatch specifically in Countering Weapons of Mass Destruction (CWMD) and WMD elimination missions. This portfolio composition and alignment works to ensure Army units are prepared for new, emerging and evolving missions in the CWMD area, establishing a start point for future force development in support of Force 2025 and Beyond. The Protection portfolio provides Soldiers with Explosive Ordnance Disposal (EOD), force protection, non-lethal capabilities, civil affairs/military information support operations (CA/MISO) and Chemical, Biological, Radiological, Nuclear and High Yield Explosives (CBRNE) equipment across the battlefield. Figure 13 displays a selected collection of capabilities as projected from current, near and extended term perspectives.

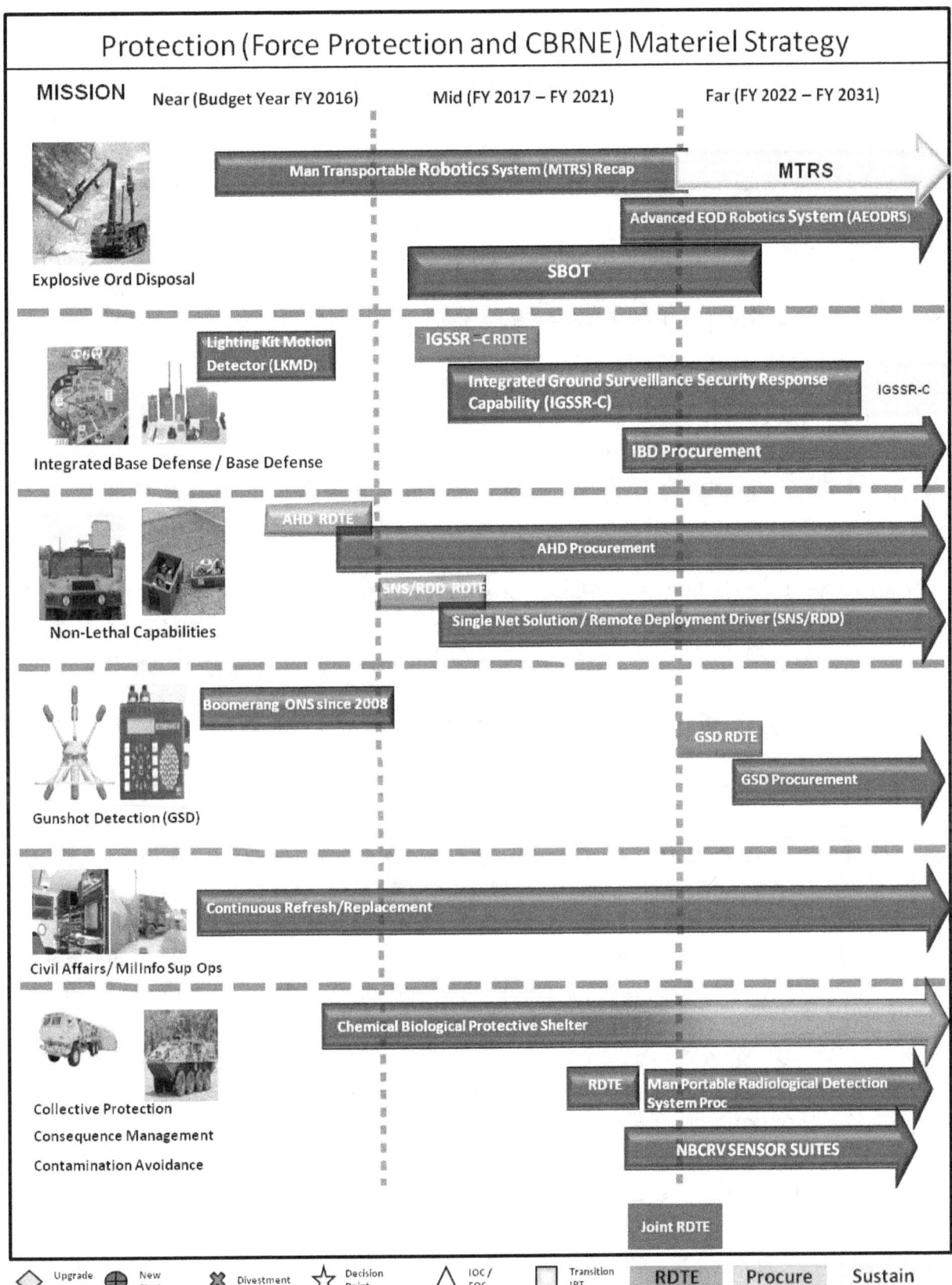

Protection (Force Protection and CBRNE) Materiel Strategy

MISSION — Near (Budget Year FY 2016) — Mid (FY 2017 – FY 2021) — Far (FY 2022 – FY 2031)

Explosive Ord Disposal
- Man Transportable Robotics System (MTRS) Recap → MTRS
- Advanced EOD Robotics System (AEODRS)
- SBOT

Integrated Base Defense / Base Defense
- Lighting Kit Motion Detector (LKMD)
- IGSSR –C RDTE
- Integrated Ground Surveillance Security Response Capability (IGSSR-C) → IGSSR-C
- IBD Procurement

Non-Lethal Capabilities
- AHD RDTE
- AHD Procurement
- SNS/RDD RDTE
- Single Net Solution / Remote Deployment Driver (SNS/RDD)

Gunshot Detection (GSD)
- Boomerang ONS since 2008
- GSD RDTE
- GSD Procurement

Civil Affairs / MilInfo Sup Ops
- Continuous Refresh/Replacement

Collective Protection / Consequence Management / Contamination Avoidance
- Chemical Biological Protective Shelter
- RDTE — Man Portable Radiological Detection System Proc
- NBCRV SENSOR SUITES
- Joint RDTE

Legend: ◇ Upgrade | ⊕ New Start | ✖ Divestment | ☆ Decision Point | △ IOC / FOC | ☐ Transition IPT | RDTE | Procure | Sustain

Figure 13. Protection (Force Protection and CBRNE) (see acronym glossary)

Section II. Strategy Update

Based on fiscal constraints, the Force Protection Portfolio procurement strategy takes calculated risk while continuing to provide the Soldier with the highest level of protection possible. EOD procurement will continue to support mobility operations throughout the close and support areas while Integrated Base Defense ties in layered protection measures to secure contingency bases. Additionally, the portfolio will support enhanced survivability across the battlefield through investment in Chemical Biological Protective Shelter (CBPS) and upgraded Nuclear, Biological, Chemical Reconnaissance Vehicle (NBCRV) sensor suites.

Section III. Portfolio Accomplishments (FY 2014 / 2015)

- Procured 74 CBPS Systems. The CBPS is a highly mobile, self-contained, rapidly deployable, chemically and biologically protected shelter that is a contaminant-free, environmentally controlled medical treatment area.

- Procured 86,090 pieces of Class 1 National Fire Protection Association (NFPA) Personal Protective Equipment (PPE) in support of U.S. Northern Command (NORTHCOM)/U.S. Army North (ARNORTH) CBRN Response Enterprise.

Section IV. Key FY 2016 Force Protection Investments

The FY 2016 Force Protection portfolio investments total $83.8M ($25.3M RDTE / $56.1M OPA / $2.4M OMA) that will ensure Soldiers are protected from multitude of battlefield and homeland security hazards. Specific investments in this portfolio include:

- $17.4M (OPA) procures 133 EOD Equipment systems. The program includes three systems comprised of the Future Radiographic System (FRS) and other systems providing EOD technicians with a rapid, reliable and secure means for identifying and disarming EOD munitions.
- $3.7M (OPA) procures 11 CA/MISO systems. The program includes systems providing essential media production and product distribution capabilities for CA/MISO general purpose forces.
- $1.1M (RDTE) funds EOD Equipment RDTE providing increased standoff distances for IED-Defeat missions, particularly for Vehicle Borne Improvised Explosive Devices (VBIED).
- $21.3M (OPA) procures CBPS Systems. The CBPS is a highly mobile, self-contained, rapidly deployable, chemically and biologically protected shelter that is a contaminant-free, environmentally controlled medical treatment area.

- $14.5M (OPA) procures Class 1 NFPA PPE in support of USNORTHCOM/ARNORTH CBRN Response Enterprise.
- $1.5M (OPA) procures Acoustic Hailing Device (AHD) systems in support of non-lethal options for combatant commanders.

SUSTAINMENT (TRANSPORTATION)

Section I. Overview

The Sustainment (Transport) portfolio provides the Army with strategic agility and freedom of movement through equipping the Total Force with Tactical Wheeled Vehicles (TWV), Army Watercraft Systems (AWS) and trailers. The role of the portfolio has evolved significantly and become more essential as adversaries and strategic competitors develop capabilities to deny U.S. access to lodgment areas.

TWVs are the workhorses within the Brigade Combat Team. TWVs support all warfighting functions and provide the combatant commander with a broad range of capabilities to include: battle command on the move, reconnaissance, communications, sustainment, medical evacuation, maintenance, recovery support, protected troop transport and a versatile platform to mount various direct fire weapon systems and fire support equipment. They are essential to the Army's mission and reside in almost every formation in the Army. The TWV fleet includes Light, Medium and Heavy Tactical Vehicles with associated trailers and the Mine Resistant Ambush Protected (MRAP) family of vehicles.

AWS are key enablers that provide multiple entry point options for forces, supplies and equipment to the combatant commander. They allow for access to shallow draft ports, inaccessible to larger strategic lift vessels, as well as access directly from strategic lift to an austere theater shoreline. These options allow maneuver forces to perform operational maneuver from the sea over strategic distances, bypass denied areas and overcome an enemy's anti-access and area denial (A2/AD) capabilities. AWS also enable coastal and inland waterway lines of communication (LOC) to increase sustainment throughput to engaged forces. These capabilities are provided by several systems including landing craft, causeway systems, tug boats and command and control interfaces. AWS at-sea transfer allow joint forces to by-pass intermediate staging bases to move from strategic shipping to tactical delivery of forces to a theater.

As depicted in Figure 14, key objectives and decision points in the Sustainment (Transportation) portfolio include:

- Joint Light Tactical Vehicle (JLTV) is the most significant procurement program in this portfolio. The Low-Rate Initial Production (LRIP) Milestone C decision and corresponding contract award for this program is expected in the last quarter of

FY 2015. Initial Operational Capability (IOC) for JLTV is currently scheduled in 4th Quarter FY 2018.

- Continue to procure modernized, armor-capable Family of Medium Tactical Vehicle for existing and emerging requirements.
- Heavy Tactical Vehicles modernized through recapitalization in both the Heavy Expanded Mobility Tactical Truck (HEMTT) and Palletized Load System (PLS) fleets.
- Continue analysis for a protected ground ambulance to replace the aging High Mobility Multipurpose Wheeled Vehicle (HMMWV) ambulances that have exceeded their Economic Useful Life (EUL).
- Develop capabilities for a Joint Tactical Truck System (JTTS) through RDT&E efforts that merge the medium and heavy truck fleets.
- Pursue development of the Light Equipment Utility Trailer and Heavy Dump Truck (HDT) to field critical requirements for organic haul capability and horizontal engineer companies.
- Continue development of automated and robotic capabilities to reduce Soldier exposure, e.g., leader/follower and automated convoy operations.
- Continue fielding MRAP to Army Preposition Stocks/War Reserve, operational units and training base.
- Continue to procure B kits, at a low production rate, to maintain the industrial base but retain the capability to surge production and leverage advances in technology.
- Modernization of the current Landing Craft Utility (LCU) fleet through Command, Control, Communications, Computers, Intelligence, Surveillance and Reconnaissance (C4ISR) upgrades.
- Sustainment of the current LCU fleet through Service Life Extension Plan (SLEP).
- Continue development/integration of Army Watercraft Strategy force protection.
- Begin RDT&E efforts for Maneuver Support Vessel - Light (MSV-L) in support of replacement of obsolete Landing Craft Mechanized (LCM). The LCM is more than 40 years old with increasing maintenance costs and aging operational capability.

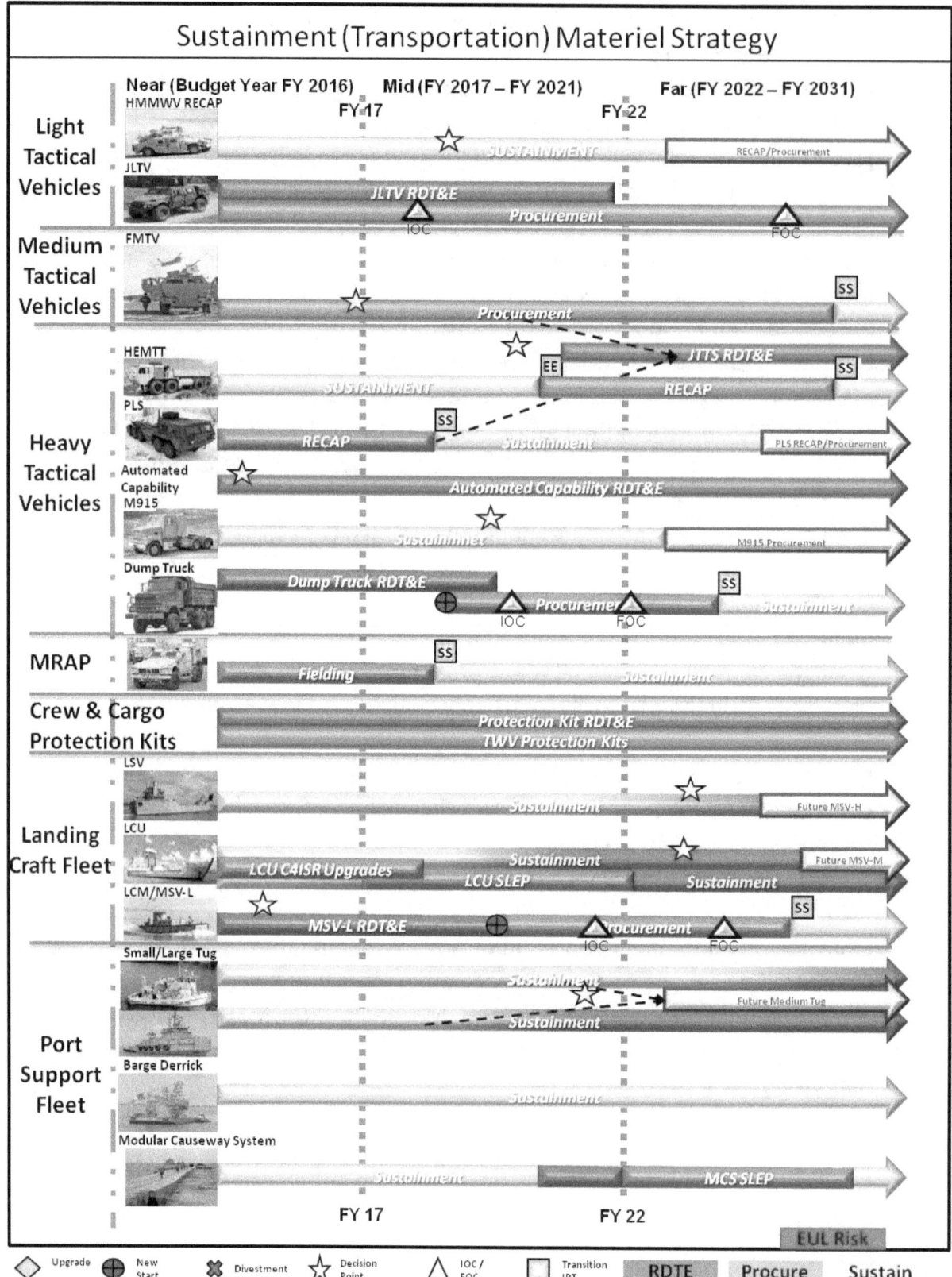

Figure 14. Sustainment (Transportation) (see acronym glossary)

Section II. Strategy Update

The Sustainment (Transportation) Portfolio equipping plan takes its priorities directly from the Army's Transportation Portfolio Strategy, approved by the Vice Chief of Staff of the Army on 30 September 2014. At the broadest level, those priorities were JLTV, MSV-L, Landing Craft Utility (LCU) C4ISR / SLEP, Soldier Protection through armor and automated capabilities, and modernization.

Top Priorities

As the number one priority, JLTV will enter Low-Rate Initial Production in FY 2015. The next critical item is to begin efforts toward procurement of MSV-L with RDT&E funds beginning in FY 2016. We will also focus on critical C4ISR upgrades and LCU SLEP in the near- and mid-terms.

Protection

We will continue efforts towards Soldier protection in several ways. The first is by continuing production of armor-capable TWVs toward the Army's goal of 50 percent of vehicles armor-capable. The next is through continued RDT&E and procurement at minimum sustainment rate of TWV Protection Kits to the Army's goal of 30 percent Armor Kits on hand. We will minimize threats by removing Soldiers from vehicles by exploring leader/follower technologies. The LCU SLEP program will provide protection for Soldiers at weapons stations on those vessels; RDT&E efforts on MSV-L and other areas will allow us to focus on Soldier protection on AWS. Bridging the effort between Soldier protection and modernization, we will continue to reset the 8,585 enduring MRAP TWVs prior to fielding, while divesting the non-enduring MRAP models through Foreign Military Sales (FMS) and other Excess Defense Article (EDA) processes.

The Army will continue analysis on a material solution to the protected ground ambulance capability gap within the IBCT and Echelon Above Brigade (EAB). To mitigate this capability gap, the Army will rely on the approved interim solution, the MaxxPro Plus survivability upgrade, long wheel base ambulances from Army Prepositioned Stocks (APS), as well as, non-material solutions to bridge the capability gap.

Modernization

Modernization across both the TWV and AWS fleet will continue. We will accomplish this through multiple lines of effort. This includes supporting the Chief of Staff's goal to increase automated capability through RDT&E on the PLS and continuing current programs to recapitalize HEMTT. In the mid- and far-term, we will examine lowering the average age across the medium and heavy fleet through RDT&E on the JTTS. JTTS may potentially reduce lifecycle costs for the Medium and Heavy fleets in

---

the long term by reducing the number of vehicle variants across the fleet, reducing fleet size and increasing parts commonality. Other low-level modernization programs include SLEP to upgrade power trains on the Army's fleet of warping tugs and a new start program, the Light Engineer Utility Trailer. We will also support modernization efforts by divesting older equipment to reduce average fleet ages.

Section III. Portfolio Accomplishments (FY 2014 / 2015)

- In FY 2014, fielded 210 MRAP All-Terrain Vehicles (M-ATV) Key Leader vehicles with improved communications suite.
- In FY 2014, fielded 7,737 Family of Medium Tactical Vehicles (FMTV) trucks and trailers.
- In FY 2014, fielded 2,528 Family of Heavy Tactical Vehicles (FHTV), and recapitalized 775 HEMTT and PLSs.
- In FY 2015, programmed to field 137 M-ATVs with improved communications suite.
- In FY 2015, the Army is projected to field, 5,334 FHTVs, and recapitalize 670 HEMTTs and PLSs. The FY 2015 FHTV budget request procures 444 PLS-trailers and recapitalizes 801 HEMTTs and PLSs.

Section IV. Key FY 2016 Transportation Investments

Total Portfolio investments are $736.3M and Key procurements are:
- $340.8M ($308.3M OPA and $32.5M RDTE) has been allocated for the JLTV program to begin Low Rate Initial Production.
- $27.5M (OPA) to procure PLS trailers.
- $127.1M (OPA) to recapitalize PLSs into armor capable configuration.
- $48.3M (OPA) to procure armor kits for FMTVs and FHTVs.
- $51.0M (OPA) for C4ISR and to maintain seaworthiness for Army Watercraft.
- $10.1M (RDTE) begins efforts toward procurement of MSV-L.

SUSTAINMENT (SERVICE SUPPORT)

Section I. Overview

The Sustainment portfolio consists of multiple systems, as depicted in figures 15 through 18, providing essential enabling capability to Soldiers. These capabilities are: Aerial Delivery (Joint Precision Airdrop Systems (JPADS)); Field Feeding (Assault Kitchen (AK) and Multi-Temperature Refrigerated Container System (MTRCS)); Field Services (Force Provider); Fuel and Water Storage and Distribution (Modular Fuel System-Tank Rack Module (MFS-TRM), Load Handling System Compatible Water Tank Rack System (HIPPO), and Expeditionary Water Packaging System (EWPS)); Mobile Maintenance (Armament Repair Shop Set (ARSS), Metal Working and Machining Shop Set (MWMSS), Fire Suppression Refill Systems (FSRS), Next Generation Automatic Test System (NGATS), Maintenance Support Device Version 3 (MSD-V3), Calibration Sets and Test Modernization Equipment); Material Handling (5K Light Capacity Rough Terrain Forklift (LCRTF)); and Medical equipment, material sets and communications (Drugs and Vaccines, Medical Field Systems (MFS) and Medical Communication for Combat Casualty Care (MC4)).

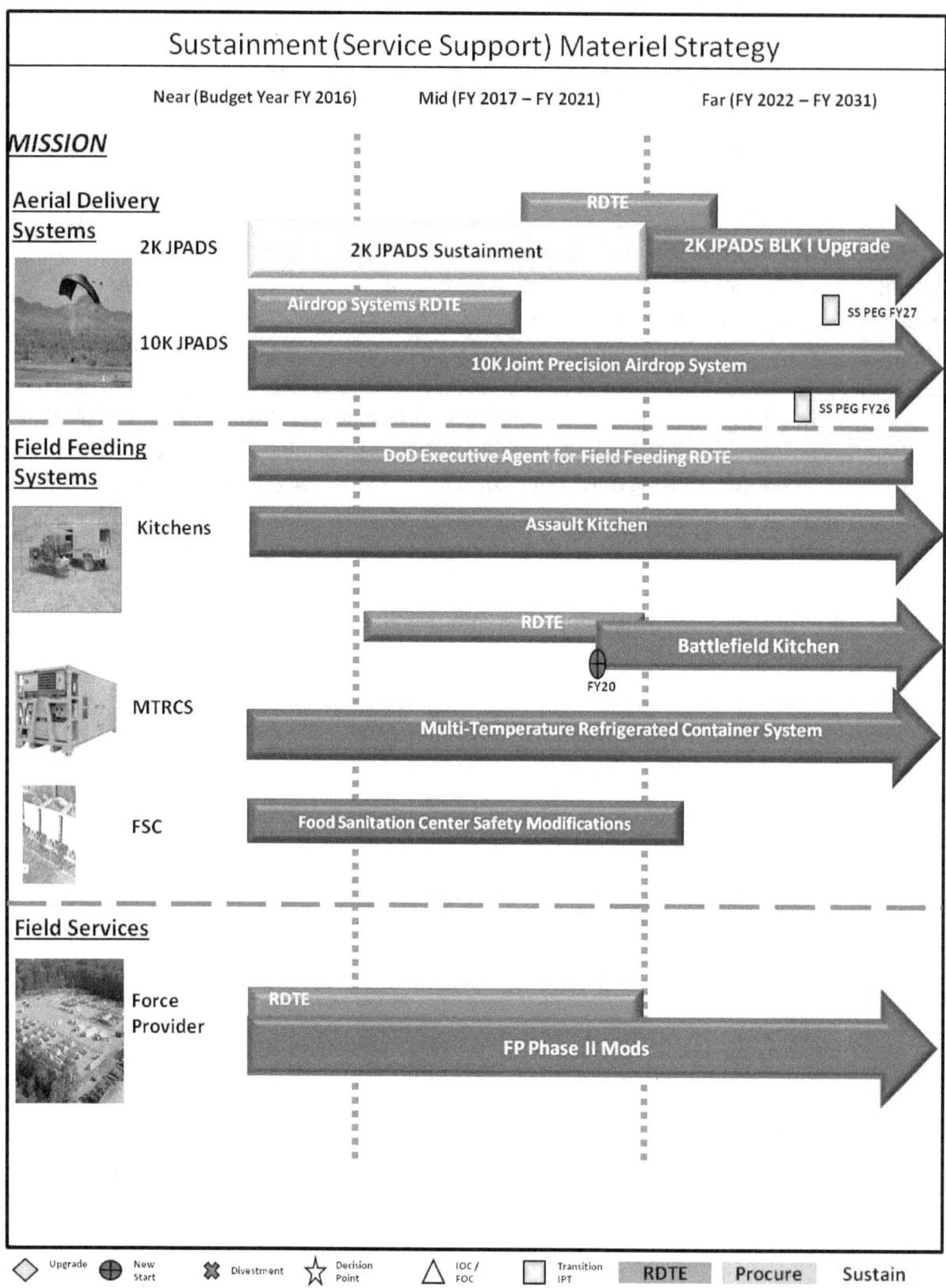

Figure 15. Sustainment (Service Support) (see acronym glossary)

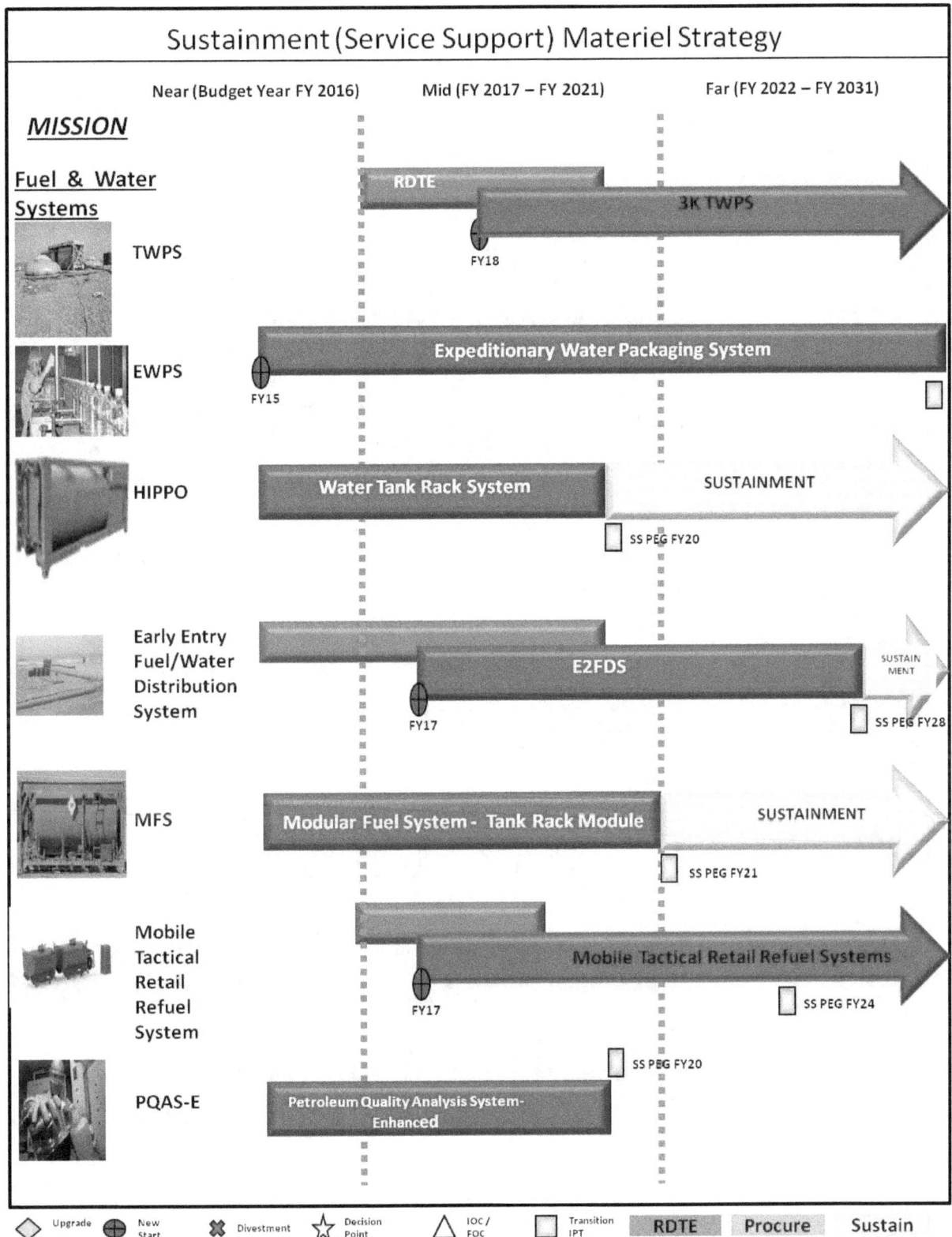

Figure 16. Sustainment (Service Support) (see acronym glossary)

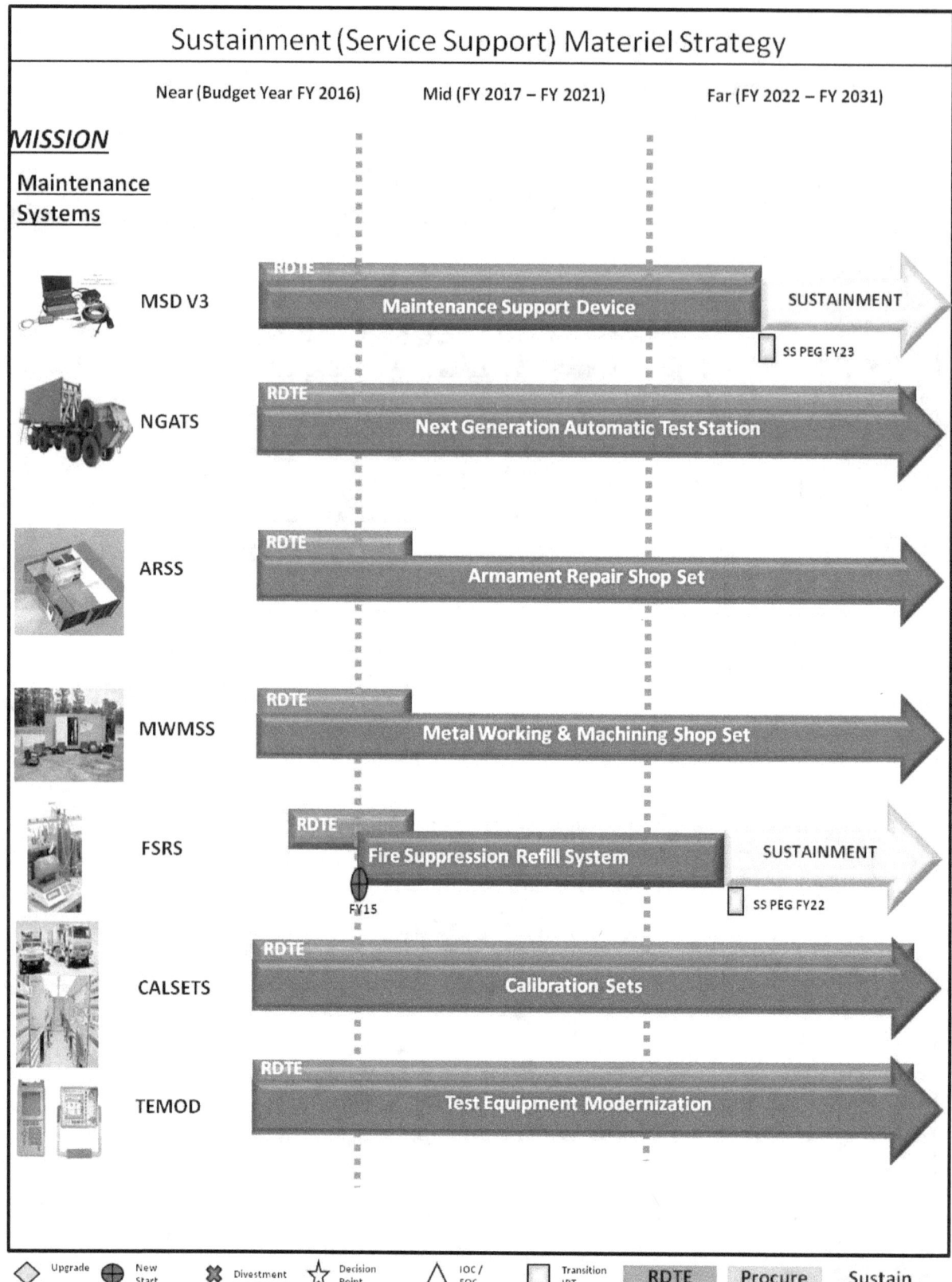

Figure 17. Sustainment (Service Support) (see acronym glossary)

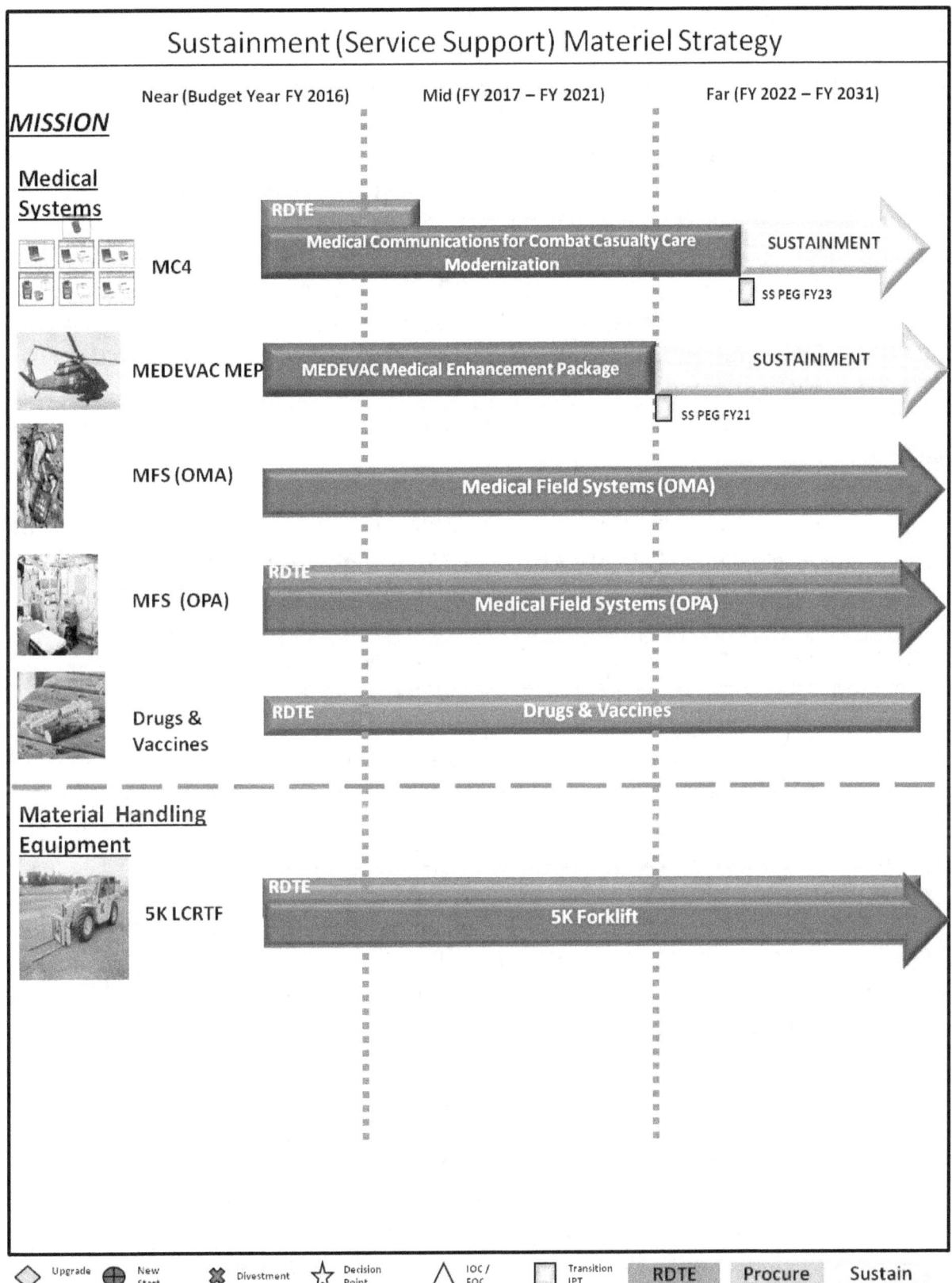

Figure 18. Sustainment (Service Support) (see acronym glossary)

Section II. Strategy Update

Based on changes in the fiscal environment, the Sustainment Portfolio strategy will maintain support to modernize the Army, but procurement is reduced to a minimum sustainment rate. We accept risk in creating longer procurement schedules to reach the Army Acquisition Objective (AAO). The portfolio funds priority medical equipment, material sets, communications and critical RDTE that support the Food and Drug Administration (FDA) regulated clinical trials for drugs and vaccines. The portfolio funds modern Force Sustainment Systems (e.g. LCRFT, 10K JPADS, AK, Force Provider energy efficiency modifications, and MTRCS); At-Platform, Off-Platform and general purpose test equipment (e.g. MSD-V3 and NGATS); priority maintenance systems (e.g. ARSS and MWMSS); and priority fuel and water distribution and storage systems (e.g. HIPPO and MFS-TRM) to replace aging and obsolete systems and reduces the logistics footprint.

Given that procurement is reduced to a minimum sustainment rate, the portfolio is challenged with meeting the following warfighting challenges: Conduct Entry Operations; Adapt the Institutional Army; Ensure Interoperability and Operate in Joint, Interagency, Intergovernmental and Multinational (JIIM) Environment; Set the Theater; Sustain Operations and Maintain Freedom of Movement; and Exercise Mission Command. The portfolio will achieve this through leveraging interdependencies with other programs and staying ahead of obsolescence in medical items, computer based systems and diagnostic and repair maintenance equipment. This will require continuous coordination, collaboration and synchronization with other portfolios.

Section III. Portfolio Accomplishments (FY 2014 / 2015)

- Fielded 1,217 pieces of medical equipment systems in FY 2014 and projected to field 2,649 medical equipment systems in FY 2015 providing medical capabilities that include dental, x-ray, lab, optometry, surgical, evacuation, preventive medicine, veterinary and combat stress control.
- Fielded 81 10,000 pound JPADS in FY 2014 and projected to procure 85 JPADS in FY 2015. The 10K JPADS provide rapid, precise, high altitude delivery capabilities to forces without the use of ground transportation.
- Procured 60 each 5K LCRFT in FY2014 and are projected to procure 148 each in FY2015. Its primary mission includes loading and unloading 20 foot International Organization for Standardization (ISO) containers in storage facilities. It's found in various units such as Brigade Combat Teams (BCT), Combat Aviation Brigades (CAB), Ordnance units, Quartermaster units and Transportation units.

- Fielded 158 MTRCS in FY 2014 and projected to procure in 64 MTRCS in FY 2015 to BCTs increasing storage capabilities and enhancing quality of life-for units operating in remote locations.
- Procured 100 each Modular Fuel System Tank Rack Modules in FY 2014 with a projected procurement FY 2015 of 474 systems providing BCTs a bulk and retail fuel distribution and storage capability.
- Procured 316 HIPPO systems in FY 2014 and are projected to procure 140 HIPPO systems in FY 2015. HIPPO provides a capability which receives stores and issues large quantities of potable water anywhere in the theater of operations. The HIPPO replaces the Forward Area Water Point Supply System (FAWPSS).
- In FY 2014, fielded 2,165 Maintenance Support Devices (MSD-V3) to improve maintenance diagnostic capability for tactical wheeled vehicles, armored weapons systems and aviation weapon systems.
- Procured 14 MWMSS in FY 2014 and projected to procure 19 MWMSS in FY2015. The MWMSS supports SBCTs, IBCTs, and Engineer Forward Support Companies by replacing 24 legacy systems with new welding and machining capabilities for the entire Army (Abrams, Bradley, Avenger, Apache, Stryker, TWV and small arms).
- Procured nine ARSS in FY 2014 and projected to procure 28 ARSS in FY 2015. The ARSS provides maintenance for the armament weapon systems of the Abrams, Bradley, Kiowa Warrior, Avenger, Common Remotely Operated Weapon System (CROWS), Apache, Stryker, and Armored Security Vehicle (ASV). It supports all weapon systems as far forward as possible on the battlefield in the ABCTs, SBCTs, and IBCTs.
- Fielded five AK in FY 2014 and projected to procure 77 AK in FY 2015 replacing legacy field feeding systems.

Section IV. Key FY 2016 Service Support Investments:

The FY 2016 Sustainment investments total $467.7M ($116.7M RDTE / $283.0M OPA / $68.0M OMA) for support programs and include fuel and water systems, load handling systems, airdrop systems, tool sets, medical systems and other combat enablers. Specific investments in this portfolio include:
- $73.8M (OPA) and $38.9M (OMA) procures Medical Devices and Medical Equipment Sets that provide health service support for Soldiers on the battle field with current standards of care.
- $24.3M (OPA) procures MC4 that supports medical information system, enabling lifelong electronic medical records, streamlined medical logistics and enhanced situational awareness for Army tactical forces.

- $16.1M (OPA) procures Modular Fuel System Pump Rack Modules to Composite Support Companies providing bulk fuel distribution and storage capability.
- $23.9M (OPA) procures MSD-V3 replacing obsolete test sets in 16 BCTs.
- $10.6M (OPA) procures NGATS replacing legacy Direct Support Electrical System Test Sets (DSESTS) and legacy Base Shop Test Facility (BSTF) in one BCT.
- $9.5M (OPA) procures MTRCS providing rapid refrigerated transport and storage of Class I items for six BCTs.
- $14.4M (OPA) procures HIPPO replacing obsolete Semi-Trailer Mounted Fabric Tanks (SMFT) and FAWPSS in Composite Supply Companies.
- $4.7M (OPA) procures calibration sets replacing obsolete calibration sets in one BCT.
- $2.2M (OPA) procures JPADS 10K in support of joint precision aerial delivery operations conducted in numerous theaters of operations/training missions.
- $17.5M (OPA) procures 5K LCRTF replacing legacy 4,000 pound forklifts throughout the Army.
- $9.3M (OPA) procures MWMSS replacing 24 legacy systems to support SBCTs, IBCTs, and Engineer Forward Support Companies (FSC).
- $10.4M (OPA) procures ARSS to support HBCTs, SBCTs, and IBCTs by providing on-system maintenance repairs to weapons as far forward as possible on the battlefield.
- $5.5M (OPA) procures Fire Suppression Refill System (FSRS) providing the capability to refill the majority of fire suppression systems fielded to ABCTs, SBCTs, and Support Maintenance Companies (SMC).
- $5.4M (OPA) procures Petroleum Quality Analysis System - Enhanced (PQAS-E) providing a Fuel Storage Testing capability for 4 Composite Supply Companies.

References

Department of the Army, 2015 Army Posture Statement, Record Copy, 05 March 2015

Department of the Army, Army Strategic Planning Guidance 2014, 30 April 2014

Department of the Army, Army Program Guidance Memorandum for Fiscal Years 2017-2021 Program Objective Memorandum, 16 Mar 2015

Department of the Army, Army Planning Priorities Guidance, POM 17-21, 29 October 2014

Department of the Army, U.S. Army Organic Industrial Base Strategic Plan 2012-2022, 15 October 2012

Department of Defense, Sustaining U.S. Global Leadership: Priorities for the 21st Century Defense, January 2012

Department of Defense, Joint Operational Access Concept v1.0, 17 January 2012

Department of Defense, Quadrennial Roles and Missions Review, 4 March 2014

Training and Doctrine Command (TRADOC) Pamphlet 525-3-1, Army Operating Concept, 7 October 2014

Training and Doctrine Command (TRADOC) F2025B Integration and Synchronization Base Plan, 30 September 2014

Acronym List

A^2/AD	Anti-access/Area Denial
AAO	Army Acquisition Objective
AAS	Armed Aerial Scout
ABCS	Army Battle Command Systems
ABCT	Armored Brigade Combat Team
ABV	Assault Breacher Vehicle
ACAT	Acquisition Category
ACFT	Aircraft Procurement, Army
ADAM	Air Defense Airspace Management (Cell)
AEB	Aerial Exploitation Battalions
AEODRS	Advance EOD Robotics System
AEP PB 16	Army Equipment Program in support of President's Budget 2016
AESA	Active Electronically Scanned Array
AESIP	Army Enterprise Systems Integration Program
AFATDS	Advanced Field Artillery Tactical Data System
AGSE	Aviation Ground Support Equipment
AHB	Assault Helicopter Battalions
AHD	Acoustic Hailing Device
AIAMD	Army Integrated Air and Missile Defense
AK	Assault Kitchen
AMD	Air and Missile Defense
AMDPCS	Air and Missile Defense Planning and Control System
AMDWS	Air and Missile Defense Work Station
AMMPS	Advanced Medium Mobile Power Sources
AMPS	Aviation Mission Planning System
AMPV	Armored Multi-purpose Vehicle
APAM	Anti-Personnel/Anti-Materiel
A-PNT	Assured Position, Navigation and Timing
APS	Active Protection System or Army Prepositioned Stocks
ARCIC	Army Capabilities Integration Center
ARI	Aviation Restructure Initiative
ARL	Airborne Reconnaissance Low
ARL-E	Airborne Reconnaissance Low – Enhanced
ARNG	Army National Guard
ARNORTH	U.S. Army North
ARSS	Armament Repair Shop Set
ASE	Aircraft Survivability Equipment
ASV	Armored Security Vehicle
ATACMS	Army Tactical Missile System
ATC	Air Traffic Control
ATIRCM	Advanced Threat Infrared Countermeasures

AW	Alternate Warhead
AWS	Army Watercraft Systems
B	Billions
BA	Budget Activity
BBA	Bipartisan Budget Act 2013
BCA	Budget Control Act of 2011
BCS-3	Battle Command Support and Sustainment System
BCT	Brigade Combat Team
BEB	Bridge Erection Boat
BFIST	Bradley Fire Support Team (Vehicle)
BfSB	Battlefield Surveillance Brigade
BFT	Blue Force Tracker
BHL	Backhoe Loader
BI/BII	Block I, Block II
BMD	Ballistic Missile Defense
BSTF	Base Shop Test Facility
C2	Command and Control
C2/SA	Command and Control/Situational Awareness
C3I	Command, Control, Communications, Intelligence
C4I	Command, Control, Communications, Computers and Intelligence
C4ISR	Command, Control, Communications, Computers, Intelligence, Surveillance and Reconnaissance
CA/MISO	Civil Affairs and Military Information Support Operations
CAB	Combat Aviation Brigade
CALSETS	Calibration Sets
CAPE	Cost Assessment and Program Evaluation
CBPS	Chemical Biological Protective Shelter
CBRNE	Chemical, Biological, Radiological, Nuclear and High-Yield Explosive
CBT	Common Bridge Transporter
CDTE	Counter Defilade Target Engagement
CE	Computing Environment
CEH	Counter Explosive Hazard
CFV	Cavalry Fighting Vehicle
CHARCS	Counterintelligence and Human Intelligence Automated Reporting and Collection System
CI	Counterintelligence
CIRCM	Common Infrared Countermeasures
CMD/CUAS	Cruise Missile Defense/Counter Unmanned Ariel Surveillance Sensor
CMD-P	Computer Meteorological Data-Profiler
CMWS	Common Missile Warning System
COCOM	Combatant Command
COE	Common Operating Environments
CoIST	Company Intelligence Support Team
COMINT	Communications Intelligence
COMSEC	Communication Security
CONOPS	Concept of Operations

CONPLAN	Contingency Plan
COP	Common Operating Picture
COTS	Commercial Off the Shelf
CPOF	Command Post of the Future
CPCE	Command Post Computing Environment
CPD	Capability Production Document
CPN	Command Post Node
C-RAM	Counter-Rockets, Artillery and Mortars
CROWS	Common Remotely Operated Weapon System
CRS-I	Common Robotic System – Individual
CS	Combat Support; or Capability Set
CS	Capability Set
CSP	Common Sensor Payload
CSS	Combat Service Support
CTE	Container Transfer Enhancement
CUAS	Counter Unmanned Aerial System
CVP	Combat Vehicle Prototyping
CWMD	Counter Weapons of Mass Destruction
DCGS-A	Distributed Common Ground System - Army
DEF SATCOM	Defense Satellite Communications
DF	Direction Finding
DFCS	Digital Fire Control System
DIVARTY	Division Artillery
DMTI	Digital Moving Targeting Indicator
DoD	Department of Defense
DOMEX	Document and Media Exploitation
DPICM	Dual-purpose Improved Conventional Munitions
DRUH-R	Dynamic Reference Unit Hybrid-Replacement
DSESTS	Direct Support Electrical System Test Set
DTI	Duke Technical Insertion
DTSS-L	Digital Topographical Support System – Light
DVE	Degraded Visual Environment or Driver's Vision Enhancement
DVE-MP	Degraded Visual Environment Mitigation Program
DVH	Double V Hull
E2FDS	Early Entry Fuel Distribution System
EAB	Echelon Above Brigade
EC2	Enhanced Command and Control
ECP	Engineering Change Proposal
ECS	Engagement Control Station
ECU	Environmental Control Unit
ECU	Electronics Controller Unit
EDA	Excess Defense Articles
EF&I	Engineer, Furnish and Install
ELES	Enhanced Launcher Electronics System
ELINT	Electronic Intelligence
EMARSS	Enhanced Medium Altitude Reconnaissance Surveillance System

EMD	Engineering and Manufacturing Development
EMIB	Enhanced Military Intelligence Brigade
EMT	Effects Management Tool
EMV	EMARSS Maintenance Vehicle
ENFIRE	Instrument Set, Reconnaissance and Survey
EO/IR/LD	Electro-optical/Infrared/Laser Designator
EOD	Explosive Ordnance Disposal
EPA	Environmental Protection Agency
EPLRS	Enhanced Position Location and Reporting System (Radio)
EPP	Extended Planning Period
ESA	Enhanced Situational Awareness
ESB	Engineer Support Battalion
ETWD	Electronic Thermal Warning Device
EUL	Economic Useful Life
EW	Electronic Warfare
EWPMT	Electronic Warfare Planning and Management Tool
EWPS	Expeditionary Water Packaging System
FA	Field Artillery
FAAD C2	Forward Area Air Defense Command and Control
FASCAM	Family of Scatterable Mines
FAWPSS	Forward Area Water Point Supply System
FBCB2	Force XXI Battle Command Brigade and Below
FCS-U	Fire Control System – Upgrade
FDA	Food and Drug Administration
FFV	Future Fighting Vehicle
FHTV	Family of Heavy Tactical Vehicles
FIFV	Future Infantry Fighting Vehicle
FISINT	Foreign Instrument Signal Intelligence
FLIR	Forward Looking Infrared Sensors
FMR	Full Materiel Release
FMS	Foreign Military Sales
FMTV	Family of Medium Tactical Vehicles
FMV	Full Motion Video
FOC	Full Operational Capability
FOS	Family of Systems
FOT&E	Follow-on Operational Test and Evaluation
FOV	Family of Vehicles
FP	Force Provider
FREHD	Forward Reconnaissance and Explosive Hazard Detection
FRS	Future Radiographic System
FS3	Fire Support Sensor System
FSC	Forward Support Company
FSC	Food Sanitation Center
FSRS	Fire Suppression Refill System
FSV	Fire Support Vehicle
FTTS	Future Tactical Truck System

FUE	First Unit Equipped
FVL	Future Vertical Lift
FY	Fiscal Year
FYDP	Five Year Development Plan
GATM	Global Air Traffic Management
GBS	Global Broadcast System
GCSS-Army	Global Combat Support System – Army
GCV	Ground Combat Vehicle
GDU-R	Gun Display Unit – Replacement
GEM	Guided Enhanced Missile
GEOINT	Geospatial Intelligence
GFE	Government Furnished Equipment
GMLRS	Guided Multiple Launch Rocket System
GMLRS-U	Guided Multiple Launch Rocket System – Unitary
GMTI	Ground Moving Target Indicator
GPR	Ground Penetrating Radar
GPS	Global Positioning System
GRCS	Guardrail Common Sensor
GSD	Gunshot Detection
GWS	GEOINT Workstation
HBC	High Band Communications Intelligence
HCLOS	High Capacity Line of Sight
HD	High Definition
HDT	Heavy Dump Truck
HEMTT	Heavy Expanded Mobility Tactical Truck
HEPPOE	Hydraulic, Electric, Pneumatic, Petroleum Operated Equipment
HIMARS	High Mobility Artillery Rocket System
HIPPO	Load Handling System Compatible Water Tank Rack System
HMDS	Husky Mounted Detection System
HMEE	High Mobility Engineer Excavator
HMG	Heavy Machine Gun
HMMWV	High Mobility Multipurpose Wheeled Vehicle
HMS	Handheld, Manpack and Small Form Fit (radios)
HMS-MP	Handheld, Manpack and Small Form Fit – Man Pack
HNW	Highband Network Waveform
HSI	Human Systems Integration
HTV	Heavy Tactical Vehicle
HUMINT	Human Intelligence
HYEX	Hydraulic Excavator
IAC	Improved Armored Cab
IAMD	Integrated Air and Missile Defense
IBCS	Integrated Air and Missile Defense – Battle Command System
IBCT	Infantry Brigade Combat Team
IBD	Integrated Base Defense
ICE	Independent Cost Estimate
ICITE	Intelligence Community Information Technology Enterprise

ICS	Interim Contractor Support
ID	Infantry Division
IECU	Improved Electronics or Environmental Controller Unit
IED	Improvised Explosive Device
IEWS	Integrated Electronic Warfare System
IF-FoS	Indirect Fire Family of Systems
IFLIR	Improved Forward Looking Infrared
IFPC	Indirect Fire Protection Capability
IFS	Intelligence Fusion Server
IFV	Infantry Fight Vehicle
IGSSR-C	Integrated Ground Surveillance Security Response – Capability
IKPT	Instructor and Key Personnel Training
IOC	Initial Operational Capability
IOT&E	Initial Operational Test and Evaluation
IOTE	Initial Operational Test and Evaluation
IOTV	Improved Outer Tactical Vest
IP	Internet Protocol
IPADS	Improved Position and Azimuth Determining System
IPADS-G	Improved Position and Azimuth Determining System integrated with Global Positioning Satellite
IPC	Intelligence Processing Center
IPDISE	Improved Power Distribution and Illumination System, Electrical
IPT	Integrated Product Team
ISIL	Islamic State of Iraq and the Levant
ISO	International Organization for Standardization
ISR	Intelligence Surveillance and Reconnaissance
ISSP	Information Systems and Security Program
ITEP	Improved Turbine Engine Program
IWS	Imagery Workstation
JAB	Joint Assault Bridge
JADOCS	Joint Automated Deep Operations Coordination System
JALN	Joint Aerial Layer Network
JBC-P	Joint Battle Command-Platform
JCR	Joint Capabilities Release
JCTD	Joint Capability Technology Demonstration
JEM	Joint Effects Model
JETS	Joint Effects Targeting System
JIE	Joint Information Environment
JIEDDO	Joint Improvised Explosive Device Defeat Organization
JIIM	Joint, Interagency, Intergovernmental and Multinational
JLENS	Joint Land Attack Cruise Missile Defense Elevated Netted Sensor
JLTV	Joint Light Tactical Vehicle
JMR	Joint Multi-Role
JNN	Joint Network Nodes
JPADS	Joint Precision Airdrop System
JPEG	Joint Photographic Experts Group

JTAGS	Joint Tactical Ground Station
JTMN	Joint Telemedicine Network
JTRS	Joint Tactical Radio Systems
JTTS	Joint Tactical Truck System
JWICS	Joint Worldwide Intelligence Communications System
KMI	Key Management Infrastructure
KW	Kiowa Warrior
LCM	Landing Craft Mechanized
LCMR	Lightweight Counter-Mortar Radar
LCRTF	Light Capability Rough Terrain Forklift
LCU	Landing Craft Utility
LEO	Low Earth Orbit
LEUT	Light Equipment Utility Trailer
LIRA	Long-range Investment Requirements Analysis
LKMD	Lighting Kit Motion Detector
LLDR	Lightweight Laser Designator Rangefinder
LOC	Line of Communication
LOCB	Line of Communication Bridging
LOS	Line of Sight
LPWS	Land-based Phalanx Weapon System
LRC	Long Range Communications
LRIP	Low Rate Initial Production
LRPF	Long Range Precision Fires
LRR	Long Range Radar
LSV	Logistic Support Vessel
LTAMD	Lower Tier Air and Missile Defense
LUH	Light Utility Helicopter
LUT	Limited User Test
LWN	LandWarNet
M	Millions
MAMI	Medium Altitude Multi-Intelligence
MAPS	Modular Active Protection System
M-ATV	MRAP All Terrain Vehicles
MC	Mission Command
MC4	Medical Communications for Combat Casualty Care
MCE	Mounted Computing Environment
MDAS	Mobile Directional Antenna System
MEB	Maneuver Enhancement Brigade
MEDEVAC	Medical Evacuation
MEP	Mission Equipment Package
MFEW	Multifunctional Electronic Warfare
MFLTS	Machine Foreign Language Translation System
MFS	Modular Fuel System; Medical Field Systems
MFS-TRM	Modular Fuel System Tank Rack Module
MfT	Multi-function Team
MFWS	Multi-Function Workstations

MI	Military Intelligence
MIPA	Missile Procurement, Army
MLRS	Multiple Launch Rocket System
MML	Multi Mission Launcher
MNVR	Mid-tier Networking Vehicular Radio
MPCV	Mine Protected Clearance Vehicles
MRAP	Mine Resistant Ambush Protected (vehicle)
MRAP-ATV	MRAP All Terrain Vehicle
MRBC	Multi-Role Bridge Company
MRBM	Medium Range Ballistic Missile
MRDS	Man-portable Radiological Detection System
MS A	Milestone A (acquisition milestone)
MS B	Milestone B (acquisition milestone)
MS C	Milestone C (acquisition milestone)
MSD	Maintenance Support Device
MSE	Missile Segment Enhancement
MSLS	Missile Procurement, Army
MSV-L	Maneuver Support Vessel – Light
MTRCS	Multi-Temperature Refrigerated Container System
MTRS	Man Transportable Robotic System
MTV	Medium Tactical Vehicle
MWMSS	Metal Working and Machine Shop Set
MWO	Modification Work Order
MYC	Multi-year Contract
NBCRV	Nuclear Biological, Chemical Reconnaissance Vehicle
NetOps	Network Operations
Nett	Not an acronym - honors World War II Medal of Honor recipient Colonel Robert B. Nett
NFPA	National Fire Protection Association
NGATS	Next Generation Automatic Test System
NGLD	Next Generation Loading Device
NGO	Non-governmental Organization
NGSW	Next Generation Soldier Weapon
NIE	Network Integration Evaluation
NORTHCOM	U.S. Northern Command
NSA	National Security Agency
O&S	Operations and Support
OEF	Operation Enduring Freedom
OFS	Operation Freedom's Sentinel
OGS	Operational Intelligence Ground Stations
OIF	Operation Iraqi Freedom
OMA	Operation & Maintenance, Army
OND	Operation New Dawn
ONS	Operational Needs Statement
OPA	Other Procurement, Army
OSD	Office of Secretary of Defense

OSRVT	One System Remote Video Terminal
OT	Operational Test
PAC	Patriot Advanced Capability
PB	President's Budget
PBUSE	Property Book Unit Supply Enhanced
PDFCS-R	Paladin Digital Fire Control System-Replacement
PDISE	Power Distribution Illumination System Electrical
PED	Processing, Exploitation and Dissemination
PFCS	Paladin Fire Control System
PFED	Pocket-sized Forward Entry Device
PGK	Precision Guidance Kit
PIM	Paladin Integrated Management
PIP	Product Improvement Program
PLS	Palletized Load System
P-MWFS	Portable Multi-Function Workstation
PNT	Position Navigation and Timing
POM	Program Objective Memorandum
PoR	Program of Record
PPE	Personal Protective Equipment
PQAS-E	Petroleum Quality Analysis System – Enhanced
PQT	Production Qualification Test
PROX/SLEP	Proximity/Service Life Enhancement Program
PSR	Precision Sniper Rifle
QCB	Quick-Change Barrel
QRC	Quick Reaction Capabilities
QTR	Quarter
RAM	Rockets, Artillery and Mortars; also Reliability, Availability and Maintainability
RCIS	Route Clearance Interrogation System
RDA	Research, Development and Acquisition
RDTE	Research, Development, Test and Evaluation
REP	Robotic Enhancement Program
RFP	Request for Proposal
RMD	Resource Management Decision
RR	Rifleman Radio
RSTA	Reconnaissance, Surveillance and Target Acquisition
RWR	Radar Warning Receiver
S&T	Science and Technology
SALT	Small Airborne Link-16 Terminal
SANR	Small Airborne Network Radio
SAR	Synthetic-Aperture Radar
SATCOM	Satellite Communications
SBCT	Stryker Brigade Combat Team
SBOT	Small Robot
SEEK	Secure Electronic Enrollment Kit
SEP	System Enhancement Package
SETA	Systems Engineering and Technical Assistance

SICPS	Standard Integrated Command Post System
SIGINT	Signals Intelligence
SINCGARS	Single Channel Ground and Airborne Radio System
SIPR	Secret Internet Protocol Router
SLEP	Service Life Extension Program
SMART-T	Secure Mobile Anti-Jam Reliable Tactical Terminal
SMC	Support Maintenance Company
SMET	Squad Multi-purpose Equipment Transport
SMFT	Semi-trailer Mounted Fabric Tank
SNS/RDD	Single Net Solution/Remote Deployment Driver
SOCOM	Special Operations Command
SOF	Special Operations Forces
SPARK	Self Protective Adaptive Roller Kit
SPCS	Soldier Plate Carrier System
SPE	Sensor Processing and Exploitation
SPS	Soldier Protection System
SRP	Stockpile Reliability Program
STARLite	Small Tactical Radar Lightweight
STORM	Small Tactical Optical Rifle-Mounted
STP	USA Space Test Program
SUE	System Under Evaluation
SUT	System Under Test
SWaP-C	Size, Weight, Power and Cooling
T2C2	Transportable Tactical Command Communications
TAIS	Tactical Airspace Integration Systems
TAIS / AWA (AV)	Tactical Airspace Integration Army Warfighter Assessment
TBC	Tactical Battle Command
TBM	Theater Ballistic Missile
TCDL	Tactical Common Data Link
TD	Technology Demonstration
TEMOD	Test Equipment Modernization
TENCAP	Tactical Exploitation of National Capabilities
TGS	Tactical Intelligence Ground Stations
THAAD	Terminal High Altitude Area Defense
TMC	Tactical Mission Command
TMiCS	Terrestrial Multi-intelligence Collection System
TOW	Tube-Launched, Optically-Tracked, Wire-Guided
TPE	Theater Provided Equipment
TQG	Tactical Quiet Generator
TRADOC	Training and Doctrine Command
TS/SCI	Top Secret / Special Compartmented Information
TSP	Tactical SIGINT Payload
TWPS	Tactical Water Purification System
TWV	Tactical Wheeled Vehicles
U.S.	United States
UAH	Up Armored HMMWV

UAS	Unmanned Aircraft System
UGS	Unmanned Ground System
UHF	Ultra High Frequency
USAR	United States Army Reserve
USNORTHCOM	U.S. Northern Command
USSOUTHCOM	U.S. Southern Command
UTR	Unit Task Reorganization
VBIED	Vehicle Borne IED
VMMD	Vehicle Mounted Mine Detection
VOSS	Vehicle Optics Sensor System
VSAT	Very Small Aperture Terminal
WIAMan	Warrior Injury Assessment Manikin
WIN-T	Warfighter Information Network – Tactical
WMD	Weapons of Mass Destruction
WNS	Wire Neutralization System
WS	Workstation
WTCV	Weapons and Tracked Combat Vehicles

April 2015

Budget numbers in this document are intended to match the President's Budget 2016 at time of submission. President's Budget 2016 is the authoritative request and this book serves to provide strategic context and program updates. For more information contact: Headquarters, Department of the Army, Office of the Deputy Chief of Staff, G-8 Future Force Division (FDF), 700 Army Pentagon, Washington, D.C. 20310. Electronic copies of the strategy are available at

www.g8.army.mil